Praise for

Will the Drama Ever End?

"Dr. McBride provides the most up-to-date, comprehensive description of the effects of a narcissistic parent on (not only) children, but all members of the family. Her clear, concise examples are engaging and demonstrate the emotionally damaging effects of this type of parenting. Dr. McBride's evaluation and treatment approach are comprehensive and effective. A must-read for clinicians working with clients affected by narcissistic parents. I don't know anyone who couldn't benefit from understanding the narcissistic influences in their lives through this revealing lens."

— **Renee Richker, M.D., child and adolescent psychiatrist**

"From the bestselling author and renowned expert on parental narcissism, Karyl McBride brings another rich and robust body of work to our resource library. For anyone who is looking to capture a deeper understanding of narcissism and the narcissistic parent and the impact of narcissistic parenting on a child's emotional experience and development, along with a clear and thoughtful 'road map for recovery,' *Will The Drama Ever End?* is a must-read!"

— **Wendy Behary, expert and author of *Disarming the Narcissist***

"In *Will the Drama Ever End?* Dr. McBride has written an outstanding book directed at children of narcissistic parents. I have followed Dr. McBride's work for years—she has been in the trenches dealing with parental narcissism in therapy and legal settings—and her insights are sorely needed. I know from my academic work the damage that narcissistic parents can cause. My hope is that this book will validate the experiences that many children of narcissistic parents have and help these adult children move outside the narcissists' psychological control and into a place that allows growth and deep connection with others."

— **W. Keith Campbell, author of *The New Science of Narcissism***

"This book makes so much sense that *everyone* should read it! Children of narcissistic parents are struggling everywhere, and this book explains why. Adult children of narcissistic parents often don't understand themselves, their relationships, or their role in the world, but this book will set you free. McBride skillfully breaks down the crazy-making family dynamics and their potential lifetime impact on the children with numerous relatable examples. Her successful five-step road map for recovery is based on her many years of experience as a therapist, as well as her own experience. Reading this book feels like a warm and understanding hug!"

—**Bill Eddy, L.C.S.W., J.D., lead author of** *Splitting: Protecting Yourself While Divorcing Someone with Borderline or Narcissistic Personality Disorder* **and developer of the** *New Ways for Families*® **parent skills training method.**

"I found Dr. McBride when I was researching background for my novel featuring a dysfunctional family based on a narcissistic mother's neglect of her daughter, Grace. As I listened to her audiobook, *Will I Ever Be Good Enough?*, I was relieved and validated that my story of Grace could be one of her cases, and happy to raise awareness of these situations. And now, Dr. McBride's new book, *Will the Drama Ever End?*, offers a handbook to those who have suffered the effects of narcissism to help them identify the trauma, reassure them of their sanity and guide them forward to heal and break free of the abuse. Brava! A welcome companion book from a brilliant therapist!"

—**Maren Cooper, author of** *Finding Grace* **and** *A Better Next*

"*Will the Drama Ever End?* is an important resource written by an expert in the field. This will assist our clients and clinicians in understanding the entire picture of narcissistic family dynamics. The abundance of real-life examples is so valuable and relatable to the reader, so they are not alone in their confusion. Dr. McBride's 5-step recovery program provides hope and empowerment for recovery."

—**Allison Brittsan, M.A., L.P.C., Psychotherapist**

Praise for Karyl McBride

"*Will I Ever Be Good Enough?* illuminates a very common and unnamed wound—the wound that results from growing up with a narcissistic mother. In this engaging book, Karyl McBride provides a clear, honest, and effective way to heal this wound and live life fully and joyfully."

—**Christiane Northrup, M.D., author of** *Mother-Daughter Wisdom,*
The Wisdom of Menopause, **and** *Women's Bodies, Women's Wisdom*

"Dr. Karyl McBride has convened a fellowship of female voices to describe every flavor of experience with maternal narcissism. However marginalized from the mainstream of mother-daughter relationships you may have felt before this, you are no longer alone on the road to recovery."

—**Sandy Hotchkiss, Psy.D., L.C.S.W., author of**
Why Is It Always About You?

"Narcissistic mothers are always there when they need you. They expect to be the center of attention, and they can be cruel if they don't get what they want. Learning how to set boundaries with narcissistic mothers is a complex challenge. Dr. McBride offers a step-by-step approach to understanding narcissism, setting limits on the abuse, and recovering from the psychological damage. This book is a must-read for every woman living in the shadow of a domineering, self-focused parent."

—**Nanette Gartrell, M.D., author of** *My Answer Is NO . . .*
If That's Okay with You

"*Will I Ever Be Good Enough?* is an amazing journey out of pain. Providing true professional guidance and clarity, Dr. Karyl McBride heaps in genuine love and kindness. This book is like having an ideal therapist at your convenience, who really helps you heal self-doubt and self-rejection. Every page is milk and honey to your soul."

—**Tama J. Kieves, author of** *This Time I Dance!:*
Creating the Work You Love

Also by Karyl McBride, Ph.D.:

WILL I EVER BE GOOD ENOUGH?
WILL I EVER BE FREE OF YOU?

Will the Drama Ever End?

Untangling and Healing from
the Harmful Effects of Parental Narcissism

Karyl McBride, Ph.D.

ATRIA PAPERBACK
New York   London   Toronto   Sydney   New Delhi

An Imprint of Simon & Schuster, LLC
1230 Avenue of the Americas
New York, NY 10020

First Atria Paperback edition March 2024

ATRIA PAPERBACK and colophon are trademarks of Simon & Schuster, LLC

Simon & Schuster: Celebrating 100 Years of Publishing in 2024

For information about special discounts for bulk purchases, please contact Simon & Schuster Special Sales at 1-866-506-1949 or business@simonandschuster.com.

The Simon & Schuster Speakers Bureau can bring authors to your live event. For more information or to book an event, contact the Simon & Schuster Speakers Bureau at 1-866-248-3049 or visit our website at www.simonspeakers.com.

Interior design by Alexis Minieri

Manufactured in the United States of America

1 3 5 7 9 10 8 6 4 2

Library of Congress Cataloging-in-Publication Data
Names: McBride, Karyl, author.
Title: Will the drama ever end? : untangling and healing from the harmful effects of parental narcissism / Karyl McBride, Ph.D.
Description: First Atria Books hardcover edition. | New York, NY : Atria Books, 2023. | Includes bibliographical references and index. | Summary: "Acclaimed family therapist and author of the classic bestseller Will I Ever Be Good Enough? presents a comprehensive and actionable guide to understanding and healing from narcissistic family abuse. A pioneer on the devastating effects of narcissistic abuse, Karyl McBride, PhD, has the answer for anyone desperate for help in overcoming the damage of being raised in a family headed by a narcissistic parent. Divided into three sections, McBride explores the insidious way a narcissistic environment is developed in a family, how a narcissistic parent damages a child's emotional growth and ability to trust, and finally, how to not only move on but become truly free. Along with an easy-to-follow five-step recovery program, plus a 33-question quiz to determine if you or a family member is displaying narcissistic traits, McBride provides understanding and hope for anyone wishing to thrive after abuse"-- Provided by publisher.
Identifiers: LCCN 2022046068 | ISBN 9781982198732 (hardcover) | ISBN 9781982198749 (paperback) | ISBN 9781982198756 (ebook)
Subjects: LCSH: Parent and child--Psychological aspects. | Narcissism. | Psychologically abused children. | Resilience (Personality trait)
Classification: LCC HQ755.85 .M42 2023 | DDC 306.874--dc23/eng/20221201
LC record available at https://lccn.loc.gov/2022046068

ISBN 978-1-9821-9873-2
ISBN 978-1-9821-9874-9 (pbk)
ISBN 978-1-9821-9875-6 (ebook)

Author's Note

The examples, anecdotes, and characters in this book are drawn from my clinical work, research, and life experiences with real people and events. Names and some identifying features and details have been changed, and in some instances people or situations are composites.

This book is dedicated to my courageous clients.
You are remarkable, spirited, daring, and inspiring.
I hold you in my heart with deep-felt gratitude.

Acknowledgments

Writing a book during a global pandemic and a divided political environment had its challenges. While it provided quiet and alone time to think and write, it also could be isolating. While I did not have the typical interaction with friends, family, and colleagues, I'm grateful for the solid support of those who stayed with me in spite of crazy times.

When writing a book, I usually choose one short mantra that continues to inspire me or keep me going, and I post it on my computer. For my first book, I used "Go after your purpose and God will give you your dream." For my second book, it was "When you do hard things, they're hard!" For *Will the Drama Ever End?*, my mantra was "This rock cannot be washed away!" The following people whom I wish to thank are also those rocks who were not washed away but stood firm with support, help, and loving encouragement.

I start with family: My children, their spouses, and my grandchildren are all special and unique people who have provided support in many special ways. You all are very close to my heart, and I always feel you with me. Thanks to all of you for your love and support. I love you more than words can begin to express.

My sister: Thanks to my little sister, who was willing to share stories and validate our own experiences growing up. You helped me on many days when you may not have even realized it. Thanks, kid, I love ya and always will!

Susan Schulman, my agent: I think often about how lucky I have been to have you as my agent throughout my writing career. I love your direct and honest approach with all aspects of our working together. I'm deeply grateful for your professionalism, integrity, kindness, responsiveness, and most of all for your encouragement that has helped me believe in myself. You have been a rock that stood firm. My respect for you continues to grow, and I will always be thankful for everything you have done for me. I also want to give a special thanks to Linda Migalti, foreign rights director for Susan Schulman: A Literary Agency. Linda, you have continued to be amazing in working with foreign translations and international agents. Thank you so much for all that hard work!

Laura Golden Bellotti, freelance editor: Laura, I was thrilled when you agreed to work with me on *Will the Drama Ever End?* I knew from our prior working together that your experience and expertise would be invaluable. It was such a pleasure to have you by my side as this book unfolded. Your unique ability to hear and keep my voice in the writing as we edit together is so appreciated. Your patience, kindness, validation, and sheer hard work will always be in the forefront of my memories of writing this book. I loved all our conversations, and you truly made this journey smooth and meaningful. You are just a lovely person! Thank you! Thank you!

Leah Miller, executive editor at Atria: My deep gratitude, Leah, for your expertise and important editorial suggestions. I really appreciated your enthusiasm and support, kind attitude, and your understanding of the sensitive material of this topic. Thank you for believing in the need for this book. It was truly a pleasure working with you. Thank you also to the entire team at Atria Books, including Libby McGuire, Lindsay Sagnette, Dana Trocker, Suzanne Donahue, Falon Kirby, Katelyn Phillips, Paige Lytle, Alexis Minieri, and Emma Taussig.

Michelle Stack, executive assistant: Michelle is the rock star who kept all the wheels turning for my businesses while I was writing the book. Michelle, you are always there with a great attitude, quick to respond, and meticulously accurate in your work. Your loyalty and being there for all our workshops, online work, and business tasks will always be so appreciated. You are the best! A special shout-out to your husband, Wendell, who has also been a great help whenever needed.

Sarah Schwallier, social media assistant: Sarah is our social media assistant who helps us keep up with social media posts, marketing, and heaps of great ideas. Thank you, Sarah, for your great work since you've been on board. I also refer to you as the "sunshine girl," who consistently remains a cheerleader, listener, and motivator with the special capacity to bring light to the room.

Sandra Molina, personal assistant: Sandra's business is called Engel Maintenance, which means "angel maintenance." Sandra is the angel behind the scenes, always there for errands, groceries, janitorial duties, and whatever else is needed. Sandra, you and your family have been a blessing to me. Thank you to you all!

Carolina Dilullo, housekeeper and friend: Lina, you're the best. You keep my house clean, which I never have time to do, but more than that our friendship over the years has been wonderful. I love you dearly. Thank you for all your support.

Chris Kitzmiller, website and IT specialist: Chris, my friend, we have seen some years together. Thanks for hanging in and being there and for everything you do for me. You are greatly appreciated.

Kate Alexander, LCSW, colleague and friend: Thank goodness I can refer to you children and adolescents who come from dysfunctional families. Your expertise as a child/adolescent therapist is outstanding. I so appreciate your deeper understanding of the complexities of the narcissistic family. I also want to thank you for your friendship and support throughout the writing of this book. Our long conversations, even if on the phone during the pandemic, kept me sane on many days. You are a dear person, and I love and honor you.

Allison Brittsan, colleague and friend: Allison, I can't keep count of all the cases we have consulted on over the years, particularly cases like those I refer to in this book. Thank you for being there and for all you have contributed to my work. I especially appreciate our early 6 a.m. conversations over coffee. It's been pretty cool even though we need to sleep more!

My clients: Thanks again to all my brave and inspiring clients who have embraced recovery and made transformational changes in their lives. You know who you are, and I am deeply grateful for being a part of each of your healing paths. This book is dedicated to you.

Contents

Introduction

In 2008, I wrote *Will I Ever Be Good Enough?* about maternal narcissism and its negative effect on daughters. I told readers that the book was not only a culmination of my years of research but also "a soul journey that took me back to when I was a little girl who knew something was wrong, feeling that the absence of nurturing was not normal, but not knowing why." The book struck a nerve both nationally and internationally. Its nineteen foreign translations have resonated with readers throughout the world.

When I wrote that book, I knew I was shedding light on a taboo topic that could lead to healing for thousands of women. I also realized there was more work to be done. Over the next decade, I heard from men and women who were desperate for guidance in overcoming the psychological damage they'd sustained from being raised in a family controlled by a narcissistic parent. *Will the Drama Ever End?: Untangling and Healing from the Harmful Effects of Parental Narcissism* is written for the millions of adults who grew up with a narcissistic mother or father and wish to move beyond the emotional injuries of the past to become truly whole and free.

I refer to a household dominated by one or more narcissistic parents as a *narcissistic family*, one in which a parent monopolizes the power by subtly and artfully denying the other members, especially the children, their personal power, integrity, and potential. Narcissism is a spectrum disorder, meaning that an individual can exhibit characteristic behaviors that are anywhere from mild to extreme. This means it exists on a continuum ranging from a few narcissistic traits to the full-blown narcissistic person-ality disorder. As you go further along the spectrum of narcissism, you encounter more problems. With that said, personal interactions always lead to some degree of diminishment for those who are in a relationship with the narcissist.

Since narcissists are self-absorbed to the extent that they cannot uncon-ditionally love, empathize with, or emotionally support another person, they are not ideally suited to be an effective parent. Selflessness, com-passion, and patience—the virtues that must come into play in order for a child to be properly nurtured and supported—are not typically found in the narcissist's emotional repertoire. As parents, narcissists generally remain unaware of their psychological limitations and the grave damage they inflict on their children.

Although much has been written about narcissism, very little has been targeted to those of us who grew up in the lonely shadow of the nar-cissistic parent. And even less has been written about how narcissistic family dynamics are passed down from one generation to the next, often becoming embedded in a family's relational DNA when left untreated. *Will the Drama Ever End?* is intended to fill this need so that readers who grew up in a narcissistic family will find a path toward ending the cycle of family trauma and rebuilding their psychological and emotional health.

I grew up in a narcissistic family where the joy of others—especially that of us kids—was a grave threat to the unhealthy parental power dy-namics that were in play. For this reason, one of my lifelong struggles has been allowing myself to experience and express feelings of joy. Like many children of narcissistic parents, I wasn't encouraged to succeed, and when I did, or when I was spontaneous, joyful, and free, my parents had an uncanny ability to rain on my parade and squash my enthusiasm, rather than cheer me on. The outcome, for me, was a learned tendency toward self-doubt, coupled with a chronic low-grade sense of hypervig-ilance, as I was always waiting for the other shoe to drop. When I was a child, any spontaneous expression of joy on my part would be met with harsh comments that were meant to turn my happiness into a sense of shame, guilt, or self-doubt. It was so confusing! I grew up with an over-whelming feeling that I'd better not be too happy or too relaxed because I never knew when something bad might happen.

My own experiences propelled me to build my career as a therapist and educator around helping others get out from under the awful legacy of inhibition and the skewed sense of self that result from being raised in a narcissistic family system. It has been my life's work to help survivors of narcissistic abuse so they may finally experience life's pleasures directly and fully.

My passion and determination led me to understand the severe harm of a narcissistic upbringing, how it misshapes families by skewing the balance of power in ways that are damaging and long-lasting for children. Most importantly, my work has led to my helping scores of people—from teenagers to octogenarians—heal and recover from this debilitating family history and begin to thrive as free individuals.

This book is divided into three parts. In Part One: *The Narcissistic Family*, you will gain a deeper understanding of: the dynamics of a narcissistic family system; how meaningful communication is hijacked; the confusion caused by spoken and unspoken family rules; why your needs didn't matter and therefore weren't met; why you are not as close to your siblings as you hoped to be; and why your family remains confusing to you.

In Part Two: *The Impact of Narcissistic Parenting*, I'll explain how narcissistic parenting inhibits a child's self-expression and the ability to trust in oneself and others. You'll discover: why emotional development is delayed in a narcissistic family; why there is an absence of trust; why the sense of self-worth is impaired; and why complex trauma is the legacy of growing up in a narcissistic family.

And finally, in Part Three: *Healing and Breaking Free*, I'll provide a proven 5-step roadmap for recovery. It will focus on: acknowledging the trauma of a narcissistic upbringing and grieving your losses; psychologically separating from your toxic parent and learning to effectively individuate; overcoming shame and guilt; discovering and honoring your authentic self; dealing with your narcissistic parent while in recovery; and finally ending the legacy of distorted, tangled love.

I am grateful to be able to share with you my knowledge, experience, and guidance as well as the inspiring stories of my brave clients who have broken free of the narcissistic family system and found freedom and joy. As we go through these pages together, I welcome you on your healing journey.

Part One

The Narcissistic Family

*We only become what we are
by the radical and deep-seated refusal
of that which others have made of us.*

—Jean-Paul Sartre

Chapter One

The Dysfunctional Dynamics of the Narcissistic Family

I always knew something was wrong in my family, but I couldn't quite figure it out. I knew Dad had the power and Mom orbited around him and everything was controlled by my father. It seemed like me and my brother were there just to make them look good. It was not until I had my first child, when I had that amazing burst of unconditional maternal love for my baby, that I realized that no one had that for me.

—Jeanette, 35

Although the specific dynamics and dysfunction of each narcissistic family are unique, all narcissistic family systems share common traits. The central characteristic is the inability of one or both parents to be fully present to the emotional needs of the children. For this reason, children who are raised within such a system have difficulty developing a strong sense of self.

Narcissistic parents come in two basic types: they tend to be either engulfing or ignoring. But the impact of these opposite styles is often the same. A child raised by an engulfing parent is so stifled that they cannot develop a healthy sense of autonomy or self, while the child raised by an ignoring parent is so busy working to gain attention that they, too, are left with a shaky or nonexistent sense of self. Both narcissistic parenting styles are marked by the narcissist's inability to see their child with any degree of love or empathy. Because a narcissist is incapable of identifying, processing, and managing real feelings, they are incapable of mirroring the feelings of another person, including those of their son or daughter.

Narcissistic parents need their children to be a reflection of their parent's worth, which means the child must present a false front of perfection in order to satisfy the needs of their parent. The child is not allowed to fail or be flawed in any way, since this would jeopardize the parent's sense of self-worth. Such a dysfunctional dynamic flips the script on how healthy parent-child relationships work: parental needs take precedence over the child's needs. So children of narcissistic parents grow up with a stunted sense of self and an inability to identify and process their own feelings. They often have difficulty trusting their feelings and building non-codependent relationships with others.

Healthy parents, on the other hand, are easily able to put their own needs aside when necessary, in order to provide consistent, loving, nurturing feedback to their developing child. Healthy parents want their children to acknowledge their own inherent worth, so they celebrate the child's uniqueness and value. And they also feel comfortable with their own feelings, which enables their children to freely express feelings and enjoy healthy relationships. This healthy relational dynamic is relaxed, accepting, loving, and flexible. Children grow up knowing who they are and that they are loved and valued. They are thus able to experience joy and build lives of meaning and depth that reflect their own sense of identity. Of course, children of healthy parents still face challenges, losses, and obstacles in life, but unlike children in a narcissistic family, their upbringing lays the groundwork for building the strong sense of self needed to meet these challenges.

What are the hallmarks of the narcissistic family? And how do we know if we're suffering from the fallout of being raised in one?

The Hallmarks of a Narcissistic Family

I've spent decades helping adult children of narcissistic parents identify and deal with the early childhood trauma they suffered growing up in a narcissistic household. There are a number of key commonalities that are present in every narcissistic family, and knowing these not only helps the adult child to realize that they are not alone but also offers concrete concepts to refer to as they navigate their way out of the tangled web spun by the narcissistic parent. Being able to identify and acknowledge these characteristics is a necessary step on the road to recovery.

No One Is as Important as the Narcissistic Parent

In a narcissistic family, every morsel of attention is usually diverted to or siphoned off by the narcissistic parent. This leaves children bereft of any positive reinforcement. Children born into this kind of hierarchy do not develop a sense of their own inherent worth or value and often spend their lives combating chronic feelings of being "less than" or "unworthy." My client Jack, twenty-eight, told me:

> I wanted love and hugs like I saw my friends get from their parents. I wanted my parents to be proud of me and so I tried to be a really good kid, not rock the boat, be the best I could be at everything I did. But whatever I did, it not only wasn't enough, it didn't seem to matter to my parents. My mom was always tired, my dad was weirdly sad all the time, and I felt unloved and alone.

Image Is Everything

How things appear is more important to a narcissistic parent than the reality of how things really are. Feelings don't matter—appearances do. Children from narcissistic families are frequently well dressed and seem to have everything, but the opposite is true: they are often profoundly devoid of parental nurturance and fail to thrive emotionally. This is another aspect of the superficiality that defines the narcissistic family. The narcissistic parent adheres to the idea that "how we look matters more than how we really are." Real feelings—messy, intense emotions that are not easy to brush off—are often forbidden. Kids who come to their parents with fear, anger, or confusion are often met with shaming. This undermines a child's natural right to feel their feelings, which is the birthright of all human beings. When my client Bonnie, thirty-one, took the scary step of calling her mother to tell her that her marriage was not working, she barely got the word "divorce" out before her mother started in: "This is not acceptable! What will your grandparents think? What will people at our church think?" What Bonnie needed was her mother to tune in to her feelings, not worry about how this would look to others.

Distorted Communication

Communication is often disjointed and intentionally confusing in a narcissistic family. There is a lot of *triangulation*, meaning rather than talking directly to one another, one person gives a message to another family member in the hopes that it gets back to the person it's intended for. Needless to say, this creates what's called *unreliable narration*. Narcissists don't want their family members to communicate openly and honestly, because then those members would be able to drill into issues, use their critical thinking skills, and call out falsehoods, exaggerations, or mistruths—in other words, call the narcissist's bluff. In a narcissistic family, communication is used as a weapon, rather than a tool.

Stephen, thirty-six, shared how triangulation often worked in his family so that his narcissistic father didn't have to communicate openly with his children or his wife:

> *Growing up was confusing. It seemed like no one in the family spoke directly to each other. My dad was the master of this. When he was upset with Mom, instead of talking to her, he either told me or my sister about it. Sometimes it didn't matter that much and it didn't bother us. But one of the worst memories of Dad venting his emotions with us rather than her was when he would tell us—more than once—that when we were grown up, he was going to move to another country and find a new wife! That really scared us. He spoke with such anger, and we were left wondering if we should tell Mom, and also what would happen to us if he did this!*

Clearly, Stephen's dad's indirect communication through his children and failure to openly discuss marital problems with his wife left Stephen and his sister with considerable ongoing anxiety.

Familial Bonds Are Suspect

In families that are controlled by a narcissistic personality, sibling closeness is prohibited or not encouraged. If siblings were able to become intimate and emotionally supportive of one another, there would be the possibility that they could form alliances against the narcissist. This violates the narcissist's unconscious need mandating that all allegiance and attention be directed to the narcissist—and no one else.

Charlotte, forty-six, has tried hard to maintain a close relationship with her older sister. But whenever they're around their mother, she manages to undermine their bond by lobbing an attention-getting bomb at one or both of them:

> *If my sister and I are having a conversation that doesn't include her, my mother will interject with things like "What are you two gossiping about?" or "Why are you saying bad things about me?" She's always wildly off base, but it always works—she manages to interrupt and put the attention back on her.*

Austin, thirty-three, told me that he has tried to stay close to his younger sister and to protect her from their narcissistic father's overbearing influence. This sibling connection does not sit well with their father, whose need for control over his children is still strong, even though they are now adults:

> *My sister calls me when she's upset about something, to reach out for support. But a few times my father has found out about our phone call, and he's pissed! He'll angrily tell me not to talk to my sister—that I'm a bad influence. He insists that my sister reach out to him, not me, and that I tell him everything she said in our phone calls!*

Children Lack Self-Trust

This is one of the most devastating consequences of growing up in a family led by a narcissist. Children of narcissists are discouraged—often aggressively and overtly (via verbal and even physical abuse) or subtly and covertly (via subtle manipulation, gaslighting, or denial) from developing and preserving trust in their own instincts and judgment. Nothing threatens a narcissist more than a fully formed, emotionally mature, and stable individual who is capable of walking away from the narcissist's drama. It becomes paramount that the narcissistic parent keep their children in a state of self-doubt so that they can be more easily manipulated and controlled. This is, in many ways, the most toxic poison in the narcissist's arsenal.

Caitlin, thirty-one, grew up with a narcissistic mother who undermined her daughter's every independent decision or action. Caitlin shared with me her difficulties in learning to trust herself:

> It didn't matter what I chose to do; no matter how noncontroversial it was, I was always met with negativity and suspicion by my mother. It's not like I was shaving my head and getting tattoos! Making the cheerleading team would trigger her saying things like "Why are you trying to hang out with the mean girls?" or "You might think this will make you popular, but it won't." It got so bad that I would question everything I did.

My client Russell, sixty, grew up in rural settings where there was only one teacher for each grade. His father was the math teacher for the high school, so when Russell had to take algebra, his father, a narcissist with resentment toward his son, was his teacher. Russell told me this sad story about how his father managed to undermine his self-confidence:

> I hated going to my algebra class because my dad was the teacher. I tried not to ask questions in class because I knew he would tease me, but sometimes I didn't understand something and had to raise my hand. When my hand went up to ask a question, Dad would respond with a smirk on his face, "What do you want, dummy?" Years later when I was in graduate school and got a B in statistics, I was really proud and wanted to share that with Dad. I called him and said, "Maybe you were wrong about how dumb I am in math," and told him about my grade. Even all those years later he still had a negative comeback. "Actually, Russell," he said, "you are a dummy in math! I think I can be the judge of that!"

The Parent's Lack of Empathy

Narcissists, no matter where they land on the spectrum, are marked by a lack of empathy. Malignant narcissists can be so devoid of empathy that they border on the sadistic and are shockingly nonresponsive when a child of theirs may be suffering. Even mild narcissists or those lower on the spectrum can wound with their thoughtlessness. Children are fragile, vulnerable creatures, and they need empathic support in order to build strength and resilience. We especially feel this lack of empathy when we're down or tired. My client Billy, twenty-four, recently told me about a shattering call he had with his father:

> *I had just had a grueling day at work and my father called and asked how I was. I didn't censor myself and told him I was feeling pretty wiped out from my day. He cut me off immediately and said, "Listen to me, Billy. You have no idea what tired is! Let me tell you about tired . . ." and the conversation became all about him. I hung up not only exhausted, but sad. Why can't he ever just forget himself for a minute and listen to somebody else?*

Tamara, twenty-one, was pregnant with her first child at seventeen and truly frightened about giving birth. She so badly wanted a mother she could talk to about childbirth and what it would be like. But she had a narcissistic mother who was never empathic with her daughter. Tamara's mother was upset that Tamara was pregnant at such a young age and had gotten pregnant before she got married. She could not forgive this transgression or provide empathy. Tamara reported this to me:

> *I got up the nerve to ask my mom about childbirth. We usually didn't talk about anything as personal as this unless it was about her. I simply asked the question "Does it hurt?" and she gave me this stern look and said, "Not really. Just think about it like someone is taking a knife to your private parts, but it won't last long."*

I wanted to cry along with Tamara as she told me this story!

The Parent's Lack of Personal Accountability

Though a narcissist may harm a child (intentionally or inadvertently), they are expert at shifting the blame for their bad behavior onto someone else or even the child themselves. This is just another of the disorder's hallmarks that contribute to the sense of unreality that permeates the narcissistic household. Vanessa, a client in her fifties, told me about her mother's lack of accountability, and how it was evident in fights over the family grocery list:

> My mother would make the list of what we needed, and my father would go to the store. Inevitably, my mom accused my dad of forgetting something that was on the list, and there would be a huge fight. But my dad always claimed he had gotten everything on her list. When I became old enough to drive, I took over the shopping and the same thing happened to me! My mother would always accuse me of forgetting an item—even though I'd have her handwritten list in my hand. I became obsessed with hanging on to the "proof" of her lack of accountability, and I still have a file folder with old grocery lists in it. It helps me remember the craziness I left behind.

The Parent's Constant Criticism and Judgment of Others

The narcissist is a person without a solid sense of self-worth who is often self-loathing. In order to prop up their fragile ego, they put others down. Narcissists are indiscriminate in expressing this behavior and often gossip about or tear down everyone from colleagues, to spouses, to their own children.

Delphine, twenty-seven, an aspiring musician, spoke of her mother's ongoing criticism of the way she spoke, expressed herself in writing, and performed on the piano:

> I wanted so much for my mom to be proud of me, but she never was. She told me that an article I wrote for the school paper was, in her words, "kind of pointless." She'd often interrupt me when I was telling her something important that happened at school with "Can't you get to the point, Delphine?" And the worst of all was after a recital that I had practiced for for months, when she announced in front of the whole family on the way home

in the car that "You should really choose something else to focus on, Delphine. You're not nearly as good as the boy who played before you."

Edward, thirty-four, told me of his father's constant put-downs of him. And he also shared this story about the habit his father had of throwing out nasty remarks to complete strangers:

My dad, although not the thinnest man in the world himself, was super-critical of overweight people. If he came across someone who was not in perfect physical shape, he couldn't hold back. Once when we were kids, he walked up to someone in the grocery store who was heavyset and taunted him by saying, "Hey! How about another donut?" My sister and I simply cringed.

Envy Is the Enemy of Love

The narcissist has an insatiable need to feel superior to anyone else, and the envy this generates overrides their ability to love. The child of the narcissist is criticized for their weaknesses and envied for their strengths, which basically obliterates the child's sense of self. The envy a narcissist feels toward a child overshadows all other parental feelings and leaves the child feeling guilty (and often ashamed) for simply being in the world. My client Aaron, fifty-five, told me this story:

A few years ago, I hosted a party for my boss's retirement. I was out back working the grill and my dad planted himself on the front porch and met every one of our guests by saying "Shitty house, don't you think?" All my friends wanted to know what the hell was wrong with my old man. All I knew was that he couldn't stand it that I had a nice house, great friends, and that we were having a party and having fun.

Josefina, forty-six, was a beautiful woman who took good care of herself. She was humble about her appearance, but her fashion, style, and everything about her were stunning. Like many women, she got her nails done professionally. People were always asking her where she shopped and who did her hair and nails. Still, Josefina had a lot of sadness and shame about the way she looked. She grew up with a narcissistic mother who was always jealous of her, constantly lashing out at her with mean comments. Josefina told me this:

> *My mother would say things like "You always know when Josefina is around because she'll be prancing around in those high heels of hers and clicking her long red fingernails on every table so people will notice her." Not only did she make fun of the way I looked, but she could never be happy for me about anything.*

The Narcissistic Injury

When a narcissist feels rejected or slighted, they are incapable of processing this perceived injury and moving on. Instead, they become fixated on any slight; consequently, those who live with them are constantly walking on eggshells, trying not to inflame the narcissist's overwhelming sense of injury. If a narcissist pegs you as someone they think will harm them, they will become vindictive and defensive, often in abusive ways.

Madison, twenty-six, told me that her mother was intensely jealous of her relationship with her father. She explained that her mom not only resented the father-daughter alone time that Madison looked forward to as a child but was also envious that Madison's dad seemed to enjoy being with Madison more than with her:

> *My mom got so upset when I wanted to hang out with my dad. Sometimes she'd pout like a little girl when I'd tell her that Dad and I were going to the park on a Saturday, or to a movie I'd been looking forward to. Or she'd give me an accusatory look and say something like "Just the two of you?" She never actually came out with the words "You love your dad more than you love me," but that was the underlying message . . . and it made me feel guilty for loving my dad and wanting to spend time with him. Thinking about it now, I think she also felt that Dad was closer to me than to her. When he and I returned from an outing, after a day when I'd had so much fun, my mom always seemed to ruin it. She'd be in a nasty mood, picking on me or yelling at me for no good reason. She just couldn't hide her jealousy. It got to the point that I wondered if it was worth the fun I had with my father to then have to face the punishment of her bad moods toward me.*

The Parent's Profound Lack of Consistency

Consistency is a hallmark of a healthy family, whereas emotional chaos and instability define a narcissistic family. This is because the narcissist is constantly projecting their unacknowledged feelings onto others. Children, especially, suffer from this lack of emotional honesty. The child often falsely interprets the parent's emotional instability as somehow being the child's fault and erroneously concludes "there must be something wrong with me if my parent is always so upset."

One of the saddest stories I ever heard was from my client Ruthie, who was in her twenties:

> *My childhood home life was, for the most part, terrifying. My father was so volatile and unpredictable that we kids spent as much time as possible away from home. But especially when we were really small, we just couldn't get away. I remember when I was seven years old, I came up with a way of calming myself down, to add some desperately needed consistency to my life. Every time I walked from the family room to the kitchen, I would stop at the threshold and blink my eyes. This gave me a sense of control that I otherwise did not have. It wasn't until I began our treatment that it dawned on me that other people didn't need to do crazy things like this, that they could just relax and feel safe in the world. That's what I want to have . . . consistency! Predictability!*

Holding Family Members Hostage to the Narcissist's Needs

The narcissist must be in control at all times, and this leads to the exploitation of others, including their children. Narcissistic parenting is often authoritarian and demanding, and the children of narcissists expend incredible amounts of energy trying to appease their parents.

Lorna, fifty-five, grew up in a household where her mother enabled her dictatorial, narcissistic father. He relished the role of family dictator and let it be known that disobeying him would not be tolerated. Beginning when Lorna was a young child, her father mandated that she fill the role of both housekeeper and nanny. Her mother went along with her husband's rules:

*My parents both worked, and it was my responsibility as a child starting as
young as eight to do all the cleaning, dishes, laundry, childcare for siblings, and
even ironing for the family. It was unrealistic for a child of my age. I still had
to keep up with my schoolwork but couldn't do it until late at night after all the
chores were done. What is weird is that I just thought it was normal and just did
it all to please them. Later, after having an eight-year-old myself, I realized how
they were totally taking advantage of me and were not concerned with my normal childhood needs. When my father laid down the rules, I obeyed . . . or else.*

The Adult Child of Narcissistic Parents

When clients come to me, they often have no idea that they were raised
within the closed system of narcissistic parenting. They might tell me of
a free-floating sense of unease that they can't pin down or define. They
ask me questions that indicate an absence of a core sense of identity,
such as: *Who am I really? Why do I feel lost? Why don't I know what I like or
what I want to become? Why do I suffer from such crippling self-doubt? Will I
still be loved if I allow my authentic self to emerge? Would I be a bad person if I
separate from my family of origin?*

When I hear these questions, I immediately get a sense of what kind
of family my client grew up in, how their childhood experience impacted
their ability to individuate, thrive, and build a strong sense of self, and
how that family history might be impacting their current relationships.
My sense of hope for their recovery kicks in as we begin the process
of untangling their family story and embracing the challenges of finally
breaking free from a dysfunctional dynamic.

Erica's Adult Story: Crazy-Making Distorted Thinking

When Erica first came to see me, she was plagued by a free-floating,
chronic sense of anxiety. She was a bookkeeper in her thirties, with two
beautiful young children, a home that she loved—and, as I soon learned,
a husband who confused her to the point of paralysis. After a few sessions, she came in and told me this disturbing story:

The other night I was home doing chores and hanging out with the kids. Tom, my husband, wasn't home from work yet. I had dinner in the oven, the washing machine going, and the kids were cuddled up watching TV when the power went out. This was about five-thirty and it was already dark out, so we were suddenly in the pitch black. I was scrambling around scrounging up flashlights and candles when Tom came through the door. He wanted to know why we were all sitting in the dark, and when I told him I'd called the electric company and was told our bill hadn't been paid, he started screaming at me: "That's a lie! I pay all our bills on time." I replied, "Well, clearly you missed this one . . ." but before I could finish, he stormed out the door yelling, "C'mon, Erica—are you going to believe some company hack or are you going to believe me?"

In fact, this wasn't the first time that Tom had neglected to pay bills without telling Erica. Although she could have come up with the extra money if he had asked her to, Tom couldn't risk damaging his pride and admitting he was short of funds, so he lied. Blaming Erica for believing some "hack" instead of him was an example of a narcissist gaslighting and manipulating reality in order to save face. Erica knew how crazy Tom's behavior was, but it still had a paralyzing effect on her. She went on:

I feel like I live in a house of mirrors. Some days things are clear and seem normal, yet at other times everything feels distorted and off balance. Every time I get even a little bit of ground under my feet, Tom will do or say something that makes reality feel really hard to hold on to.

The shame Erica felt as she told me this was palpable. I held eye contact with her and told her that she was not crazy. It was clear to me that she was living in a family that was being held hostage by her immature and narcissistic husband. We now had something very concrete to work with. I knew I could help Erica regain her center of gravity and her trust in her own judgment, and that with some hard work and insight she'd be able to relax and enjoy life on her own terms.

The basic scenario of the "lights out" episode that Erica shared with me is a classic example of the dysfunctional dynamics in a narcissistic family system. Tom, the narcissist, was incapable of being honest and responsive about what was clearly right in front of him: his family was sitting in the dark! All he could experience was the blow to his own ego when Erica pointed out the simple truth: he had neglected to pay the electricity bill. Like most narcissists, Tom's ego was incredibly fragile. Any perceived slight or threat to his position as "head of the family" triggered either a tantrum, the silent treatment, or, in this case, a crazy-making display of distorted thinking.

How is it that Erica was blindsided by Tom's irrational behavior? She was a competent woman, had put herself through school and boot-strapped her way to a successful job as she was raising two children under the age of five. While Tom's irrational outburst and denial of respon-sibility were undeniably crazy, most often his means of manipulating Erica was much more subtle, often triangulating their relationship by positioning her against her children or someone else she felt close to. His bottom-line objective was to get Erica to question her own sense of reality. The obviousness of an unpaid electric bill resulting in the black-out—and Tom's brazen display of narcissistic pettiness—allowed Erica to finally get that she wasn't the problem after all.

Living with a narcissist is like being in a boat in the middle of a peace-ful lake in which the narcissistic ego, like an underwater sea creature, is constantly causing upheaval in the boat. Those in the boat can't quite detect the source of the problem, but they know that the lake would be calm if it weren't for the often subtle yet unsettling disturbances.

What is missing from the passengers in the "boat"—the narcissistic family system—is an acknowledgment of the source of the waves. The family needs a sense of why this is happening that is consistent with reality. The emotional turbulence caused by Erica's husband's denial of reality is what kept her from gaining a solid emotional footing, and it is what kept her subconscious mind on constant "high alert." This lack of consistency between reality and Tom's denial and concealing of reality was the source of her self-doubt and anxiety.

My job was to explore Erica's childhood with her to see if there were factors that may have contributed to her being drawn to a narcissist when it came time to establish her own family.

Erica's Childhood Story—Mom Needed All the Attention

Erica grew up with a younger brother, Ben, in a small town. Her home was on a block brimming with young families. There were always neighborhood kids around to play with, and the sidewalks were alive with sounds of laughter, dogs barking, kids calling out to each other. Front lawns were strewn with bikes and soccer balls, and groups of kids would stop and wave at passing cars.

At home, it was another story. Erica's mother was emotionally fragile and prone to psychosomatic illnesses that rendered her bedridden for days and helped her gain the family's focused attention. The blinds in the house were often pulled tight, and both kids became adept at tiptoeing over the creaky places in the home's hardwood floors. Erica's father, when he wasn't away at work—which was often, including long business trips out of state—tended to his wife as though she were on her deathbed.

Erica described to me how all life seemed to end at her doorstep, and that once she got home and opened the door, her heart would sink when she entered the muted atmosphere of her house. She would go from being a vibrant, popular member of what she referred to as the neighborhood "sunshine kids" to coming home and feeling like she would fade and disappear.

From an early age, Erica learned to hide her own feelings, knowing that her father and mother were both utterly consumed with her mother's feigned illnesses. Her needs were ignored so her mother could receive the attention she demanded. Erica explained:

I knew that asking for help would be met with disdain and harshness. Every request, even if it was for something as simple as needing a signature for a school field trip, was met with exasperation. It was as if I was always just too much for them. They hated being bothered by me or Ben, so I essentially became his caretaker. The two of us were like refugees in our own home.

When I asked Erica if she thought her parents loved her, she responded, "Of course!" But over time, as I helped her to realize that love is a verb and is expressed by selfless acts of kindness, attention, acceptance, and consistent nonjudgmental support, Erica realized that perhaps a force more powerful than love had dominated her early family life.

The life-stunting power of the narcissistic parent kept both parents from being truly available to lovingly parent Erica and Ben. Neither child had the support they needed to really grow and flourish. Erica's mother's narcissism created an environment of abject, albeit quiet, ignoring and neglect. Her father could have been a counterbalance to his wife's absence-in-place, but he was too bonded to her and her narcissistic needs to make himself available to his children. The net result was that Erica and her brother were essentially left to raise themselves.

It was no wonder then that Erica was drawn to someone like Tom. She came from an ignoring, narcissistic family where her needs were not heard or seen, and she learned to be invisible so that she didn't cause problems. She learned with Tom that if she did what he wanted and never spoke up for herself, all was good; but when she needed to speak up, all hell broke loose. It was a familiar pattern to her. It's interesting how we are attracted to the familiar until we really work our recovery.

John's Story—An Extension of My Father

The style of narcissism that plagued John's family was overt and all-consuming. An only child, John was utterly taken over and engulfed by his father, John Sr., who, from the moment of John's birth, viewed his son as an extension of himself. John became the avatar for all of his father's missed opportunities and perceived social slights, and from an early age, the pressure was on for him to be "the best John he could be." John, twenty-five, told me:

> I was always a straight-A student, a star athlete, and the rest of my schedule was packed with high-prestige activities, like being the editor of the school newspaper. But by my senior year in high school, man, I was exhausted and utterly hollowed out inside, and I had no idea why. I just felt like an impostor, a fraud.

John had grown up craving the love and admiration of his father, who gave it freely only when John offered him proof of his worthiness: a stellar report card, a mention in the sports section of the local paper, or some other sign that the outside world acknowledged John's value. Only then would his dad bother to express approval of his son.

For his father, "failure was not an option," so John grew up believing that he wasn't allowed to make mistakes, change his mind, or in any way veer "off track." This put so much pressure on him that when he finally went off to the fancy Ivy League college his father chose for him (one that John Sr. could not get into himself), John was so depressed that he was unable to function. He had to leave school after one semester, and when we started treatment together, he had no idea who he was, why he was going to college, or where he fit into the world. John had been so en-meshed with his engulfing father that he had never been given the space and support he needed to build a solid, individual identity for himself. Instead of nurturing him, John's narcissistic father had consumed him.

John's and Erica's stories may seem like polar opposites—one a por-trait of covert ignoring and neglect, the other of overt engulfing suffoca-tion. Their parents represent the two styles of parental narcissism, but both experiences result in offspring who lack the nurturing and uncondi-tional love necessary to develop an authentic sense of self.

Two Styles of Parental Narcissism: Covert and Overt

Overt narcissism is more easily detected, as its features include an over-whelming display of grandiosity, an inflated sense of self-worth, boast-fulness, arrogance, entitlement, and a preoccupation with fantasies of success. Such behavior may be what most people think of when they hear the word "narcissist."

The way that Charlie, sixty, describes his mother clearly fits the defini-tion of an overt narcissist:

My mom is completely focused on herself and expects the world to revolve around her. She talks about herself and her accomplishments incessantly to anyone who will listen. If you attempt to interject your thoughts or ideas or experiences, she has a way of utterly ignoring what you've said and immedi-ately turning the conversation back to herself. She's exhausting to be around.

When Charlie was a child, his mom behaved in much the same way—throwing the attention back on herself, never focusing on her son's concerns or accomplishments. Although he told me that he always wanted a mom he could talk to about his feelings and from whom he could gain comfort and solace—and someone who could be proud of him—he learned early on that was not happening:

I remember coming home from school upset about something that happened and trying to talk to my mom. She would interrupt me, ignore what I was saying, and start talking about herself, because whatever I was telling her reminded her of her own experiences. And she could never give me credit for the good things I did. She would immediately start talking about when she was a kid and how great she was at everything.

Covert narcissism is more hidden, because the narcissist's demeanor is more reserved. Theirs is a smug, subtle sense of superiority. The covert narcissist can be quietly manipulative and passive aggressive but still will attempt to make things go their own way. Sharline, forty-two, describes her father:

Dad rules the roost in a quiet, authoritarian manner. He's stern and shaming at the same time. He can give you that look, and you know you're in trouble for something. He manipulates with the silent treatment, pouting and brooding, but you always know that he's upset. You would have to live with him to realize this. When I was growing up, whenever I expressed interest in anything, he quietly dismissed it with a put-down. I really wanted to take piano lessons, but he thought that was a waste of time, probably because he wasn't into music himself. If I brought it up, he would just stare into space or give me that look of disbelief like I was stupid to even mention it. Even now, when I have a good job that I find fulfilling, he still tries to subvert my sense of independence by disagreeing with my choice of career. He wanted me to be an engineer like he was, so me choosing to be a kindergarten teacher is not good enough for him. When I start to talk about my work, he finds an excuse to walk out of the room.

Both covert and overt narcissists are envious of others, have a fragile ego, lack empathy and the ability to tune in to others' feelings, are interpersonally exploitative, and believe that they are special or unique.

The impact of both styles of narcissistic parenting is the same: the child grows up without a strong sense of self, and without any real experience of what healthy love and intimacy look or feel like. It's no wonder that children of narcissistic parents often recreate a version of their own dysfunctional family system when they set out to start families of their own. Learning about one's family origins and understanding the dark legacy of narcissistic parental love are what will free Erica, John, Charlie, Sharline, and legions of others from replicating a narcissistic family tree.

Moving On ...

In this chapter we've explored some of the dysfunctional dynamics of the narcissistic family to help you get a handle on the psychological makeup of such a family: distorted communication, the focus on image, the child's lack of self-trust, the narcissistic parent's lack of empathy and accountability, and their insistence that their needs always come first.

In Chapter Two, we'll look more closely at the narcissistic family's distorted communication patterns.

I realize that this is a lot of tough material to absorb, but learning as much as you can about the complexities of parental narcissism will help you get past what you may have inherited from an unhealthy family system and onto a healthy path to recovery.

Chapter Two

Distorted Communication

I never learned how to stand up for myself and communicate directly. In my family of origin, I was shamed and humiliated when I had an opinion that differed from those of my parents. To this day, when I try to talk about things I didn't like about my childhood, they tell me I'm crazy and that the things I know happened didn't happen. They say it's just my sensitive nature and my imagination.

—Carlos, 43

Communication is a wide-ranging topic about which entire books have been written. It is our way of connecting with others and crucial to all intimate relationships. Healthy communication should be open and relaxed, reciprocal and respectful. It involves careful listening and reflection and acknowledgment of the other person's feelings. In a healthy relationship, you should feel comfortable being your authentic self and expressing the real you. The most rewarding communication with others brings out the best in you so that you can shine and be celebrated.

There are various ways in which we communicate with others, including verbal, nonverbal, written, and visual communication, as well as communication through our actions. In order to live, work, and play together, members of a family must communicate effectively with one another. In healthy families, interactions are kind, direct, honest, and display mutual understanding and support.

In narcissistic families, communication is anything but direct. Keeping the system off balance and creating confusion and hurt are prized more than honesty and understanding. In this chapter, we will discuss the dysfunctional communication techniques found in the narcissistic family. Hang on, this isn't fun.

Gaslighting

The term "gaslighting" became popular from a stage play that eventually became a movie titled *Gaslight* in 1944.[1] The movie was about a woman married to a controlling and manipulative man who was secretly attempting to convince her she was crazy. He would dim the gaslights, and when she noticed, he would say they were fine, and she was imagining things. Gaslighting is a sneaky kind of psychological and emotional abuse, and the effects can be devastating. It is used by abusers as a way to make you doubt your own reality and truth and begin to question your own sanity.

Narcissists commonly use gaslighting to help them remain in control. If they can make you feel uncertain, anxious, and incompetent, they can then more easily control you. What a horrible thing to do to anyone, but particularly to your own children as you raise them. Obviously, good parents would want their children to trust their own feelings, as well as to feel strong, competent, and sure of themselves.

The most common evidence of gaslighting that I notice with my clients who were raised by a parental narcissist shows up when they attempt to criticize a parent's past behavior. The narcissist's fragile ego doesn't allow them to deal well with confrontation or accountability. I usually discourage such confrontation by my patients, because a narcissistic parent's inability to be accountable for their behavior generally results in the adult child's continued pain, disappointment, and angst.

My client, Jody, forty-nine, told me this about her confrontation with her mother:

I was so excited to have worked hard on my recovery in therapy. I felt strong and ready to get things off my chest with my mother and let her know that I now understand that she was abusive to me growing up, both physically and emotionally. I don't know what I expected, but it did not go well! She sat there smugly and listened for a few seconds and then cut me off and told me to get out of her

house or she would call the police. She said that none of what I was saying was
remotely true. Her final words as I left the house were "I was the best mother you
could ever have had!" I was in shock and felt like I was back in a PTSD collapse.

Many of my clients want to engage in this level of confrontation, but it rarely goes well, which is why I advise against it. As we will see in Part Three: *Healing and Breaking Free*, recovery is an inside job, which doesn't involve confronting or changing your parent.

Other forms of gaslighting involve the parent saying that they don't remember things the way you do or telling you that you're too sensitive. Mark, forty-three, recalled conversations with his father:

Whenever I tried to talk to my dad about my feelings about my childhood, he
would always tell me I was the sensitive one in the family, the one who could
never be happy. He would usually end the conversation with "I hope someday
you will find happiness!" The reality was and still is . . . I am happy and have
a good life now, but that could never be acknowledged by my dad. My having
a good life despite my childhood experiences is just too threatening to him.

Nadia, thirty, recalled several instances when, due to his gaslighting technique, her father made her and her mother feel as if they were the crazy ones:

When I was about fifteen, my dad hadn't come home on yet another eve-
ning, so Mom and I went looking for him. We saw him going into a nearby
bar with a woman. He didn't see us, so we went home and waited for him to
return. When he got home, he lied and said he was working late. My mom
didn't want to stir things up at the time, but we both knew what we saw.
Another time I was with friends at a local movie theater, and he was sitting
in the back row with another woman. I could tell he saw me but neither
of us said anything. I was humiliated in front of my friends, but the next
morning at breakfast I told him I'd seen him at the movies. He told me I was
crazy and actually laughed about it. That was just his way.

Just like in the movie *Gaslight*, many of my clients have been driven to question their own sanity when a narcissistic parent dismisses their account of what really happened with a lie. I reassure them that they are most definitely not crazy. What they are experiencing is a crazy-making behavior known as gaslighting—a controlling technique employed by the parental narcissists in their lives.

Triangulation and Indirect Messaging

Healthy communication involves relaying a personal message to someone by talking directly to that person. Triangulation, on the other hand, is a form of indirect communication. In narcissistic families, it is common for one family member to talk to a second family member about a third family member—rather than two people talking directly to each other. The message eventually gets back to the person it's intended for, but it is often distorted—similar to the old childhood game of telephone.

There is a clear difference between healthy and unhealthy means of communicating: a straight line of direct communication versus a triangle of indirect communication. Why would a family member use triangulation to get their message across? Because that person has learned to be dishonest and indirect in an effort to safeguard their own feelings from being hurt. Or because they've experienced how expressing their feelings can initiate fights, so they find it safer to communicate through another person. Such passive-aggressive behavior can be a way to hurt someone indirectly. If someone is angry at another family member, they can vent that anger while not dealing directly with the person they're angry with. Of course, nothing gets solved this way. Problems are not dealt with, and an unnerving sense of tension hangs in the air.

Candace's triangulating behavior is a case in point. At sixty, Candace was very angry with her daughter, Lana, thirty-two, but chose to communicate her anger indirectly. Here's what happened: Candace had prepared a holiday meal for the extended family, and Lana called at the last minute to say she couldn't make it because she wasn't feeling up to it. Lana's three children were also invited, so now they would not be coming either. Instead of calling Lana directly to tell her how hurt and upset she was, Candace spent the entire day ruminating and telling the rest of the family how inconsiderate and rude Lana was. Candace was clearly hoping her remarks would get back to Lana and make her feel guilty. Sure enough, Lana's brother called her the next day and told her how their mother was gossiping about her all day at the holiday party. Lana was hurt that her mother would talk about her like this with the whole family. She also spent days feeling guilty, but she and her mother never had a direct conversation about this event. The next time they were together it was as if nothing had happened. Lana and her brother knew that discussing it would just cause more problems because their mother would deny it.

Olivia, forty-four, was a narcissistic mother who was upset about her twenty-year-old son's addiction to alcohol and his problems in life as a consequence. She was especially concerned with how his behavior cast her in a negative light as a mom and how it reflected poorly on the family's reputation in general. Rather than directly talking to her son and encouraging him to seek help, she vented her displeasure by disparaging him to her other son, Griffin, twenty-two. Griffin gave me his take on his mom's indirect messaging:

> *Mom seemed mostly concerned with how my brother's problems looked to other people. I hated hearing her put my brother down, even though I knew he had a problem. But it didn't surprise me. She was always talking behind people's backs. The fact that she came to me to complain about how upset she was but couldn't talk to my brother to see what was going on with him? It's kind of a sad situation.*

Triangulation clearly does not solve problems but keeps drama in the air for everyone. It creates more distrust and a lack of safety, because people in the family talk behind each other's backs instead of directly trying to solve whatever issue is at hand.

Projection

Projection is the process by which a person takes their own emotions and transfers them onto another person. Narcissists don't embrace and deal with their own feelings; they project them onto others. So if the narcissistic parent is the one who is feeling angry, it would be common for them to say to their child, "Sofia, why are you feeling and acting so angry today?" When this happens, Sofia would feel like the remark is coming from out of the blue because it has nothing to do with her. Can you imagine how confusing this is to a child? Of course, they will internalize the situation and feel like there is something wrong with them, even if they have no idea what just happened. In this way, children of narcissists often become scapegoats for the parent's self-loathing and unhappy lifestyle.

Projection is also apparent when a narcissistic parent accuses his child of a behavior relating to the parent's own shortcomings. For instance, if a father feels deficient in some way, he might repeatedly call his son clueless or ignorant. Or a mother who has failed to put forth sufficient effort to succeed in her career might accuse her teenage daughter of being lazy.

In the following story, Calvin, fifty, told me about his mother's unacknowledged behavior, and the projection was clearly evident:

Believe it or not, my mother was a thief. I am convinced she was a kleptomaniac but was left untreated. We never said anything, but when we were kids, she was constantly taking things from Walmart and grocery stores. That was bad enough, but she blamed us for it, calling us thieves, and we would get in trouble for something we didn't do. It was way too confusing to even explain. We all saw what was happening, but we didn't have the nerve or the power to go against her word.

You wonder how little kids survive with this kind of insidious abuse.

Another example of projection: Kayla's mother, fifty, believes she knows everything that Kayla, twenty-five, feels and constantly tells her and other people such untruths as "Kayla hates this . . ." and "Kayla would never want to do that. . . ." Most of the time these statements are a projection of the mother's feelings and not at all true for Kayla. For instance, when Kayla started a new job as a social worker, her mother's first remark was "And you don't even like people!" In fact, Kayla is outgoing and sociable, so her mother's remark couldn't have been further from the truth. When Kayla figured out that her mother's incorrect pronouncements about her were mostly projections of her mom's own attitudes and feelings, the pieces of the puzzle about her family started to come together rather quickly. That realization has led to Kayla's beginning to feel relief and self-validation.

Shaming and Humiliation

What better way for a narcissistic parent to shut down their child's inclination to speak up than through shaming and humiliation? These common tactics keep family members walking on eggshells, ensuring that the parent remains in control. A narcissist's fragile ego and self-loathing drive their need to project those humiliating feelings onto others. Shaming and humiliation are forms of emotional abuse, and they can be manifested in a verbal put-down, a mean look, a gesture, or by simply dismissing the person and walking away.

An especially hurtful tactic that I've seen narcissistic parents use to shame their children is to punish them publicly on social media. I was interviewed about this issue in 2018 by the *Sun*, a UK newspaper. The editors had found several videos online of parents punishing their children by shaming them on the internet. They gave examples of videos showing parents driving over Xboxes, setting Christmas gifts on fire, or shaving the child's head or giving the child a weird haircut and then saying such things as "You will stay this way until you behave better at school." It was shocking to see the number of hits these videos were getting. I shared my perspective with the *Sun*:

> *Not only is this emotionally abusive, but it causes young people to grow into adults who suffer with crippling self-doubt, fear, and anxiety that do not go away. Children respect those who respect them and their tender feelings. If you want a child to become a kind, loving person who is able to provide empathy in relationships and parenting, you have to give that to them first.*[2]

It may be hard for others to believe, but sometimes children of narcissists are shamed and humiliated for doing good things. Jennifer, fifty-two, told me that it was difficult for her to feel proud of herself for her accomplishments because her narcissistic mother always made her feel ashamed:

> *I often was awarded academic prizes in science when I was in middle and high school, but when I told my mom, her only response was "Don't get a big head—and don't talk about it with other people or they'll think you're bragging." Rather than being proud of me, Mom seemed angry with me for even mentioning the award. I learned to keep my successes to myself.*

Why did Jennifer's mother need to shame her daughter for winning the science awards? Because this narcissistic parent could not tolerate her daughter succeeding in ways she was never able to.

Jake, forty, reports that one of his father's favorite sayings to him growing up was "Who do you think you are?" This typically occurred when Jake was just being himself and having fun. If Jake's behavior did not meet with his dad's approval for whatever reason, he would be cut down a few pegs by that rude question. Jake shared with me that as a child, he didn't really understand what his dad meant by it, but he finds that the question continues to thwart him:

> *I used to like to tell jokes and try to be funny with my friends in silly ways. It felt good to laugh and be goofy sometimes. But my dad was a humorless, negative, crusty old guy and couldn't stand it if I was acting happy or just having some fun. It always hurt me when he'd say "Who do you think you are?" because I didn't think I was anyone special, I was just having fun—or trying to, anyway. But he made me feel ashamed of being happy. Now I still catch myself holding back from being myself with people.*

Sarah, forty, constantly heard from her narcissistic mother the common yet inappropriate phrase "What is wrong with you?" If a parent asks this question with a compassionate tone, wondering if the child is troubled or not feeling well and offering an opportunity to share their feelings, that's a good thing. But with narcissists this question is typically used in exasperation and in a shaming way that indicates a defect in the child. When a parent—the person upon whom the child is dependent for everything—indicates that something is wrong with the child, that child will internalize the comment and believe it. They will ask themselves "What *is* wrong with me?" and will struggle to find an answer. They may rely on their limited experience and knowledge and come up with something that could be wrong with them. In this way, children of narcissistic parents can internalize the negative message that "I am not good enough" or "I am a bad person." The shame then becomes persistent and difficult to overcome.

Sarah told me:

> *The message I got from Mother was that nothing I did was right or okay. She could never compliment me on anything or tell me I'd done a good job on something that meant a lot to me. There was always something I needed to do better, much better. So I could never relax. I walked around in a state of hypervigilance, waiting for what she'd say next that would make me feel incompetent. I was always afraid I would make a mistake.*

Mandy, forty-five, grew up with a narcissistic mother who demanded praise for everything she did, including her cooking. Her father would offer over-the-top compliments, such as "Wow, another five-star meal, honey!" and the rest of the family would chime in with their flattering approval. Mandy's role was exclusively cleanup, as her mom never taught her how to cook. As an adult, Mandy eventually learned how to prepare a meal, but whenever her parents came to visit, she realized that their belief was that she was a horrible cook. She would try really hard to please her mom and dad by preparing special dishes, but she suffered from her mother's cruel teasing: "I guess you didn't inherit my cooking genes!" Given her history of having been sidelined and diminished by her mother, Mandy believed the negative comments and bought into her mother's shaming of her.

It took our work together for Mandy to begin to untangle that negativity. During one therapy session, she showed me a picture of a plaque she had put up on her kitchen wall that read: "Most people have eaten in this kitchen and gone on to lead normal, healthy lives." I complimented Mandy on her insight and sense of humor.

Sadly, there is great power in shaming and humiliation. If a parent engaged in this behavior toward you as a child, you understand how it can shut you down emotionally and cause you to doubt yourself. It is especially traumatic when it happens to children who are just beginning to learn about interpersonal relationships. William, twenty-nine, reported this distressing story of being humiliated by his father when he was in middle school. My heart ached for him:

> When I was a kid, my dad was just plain mean. I wasn't a perfect kid, granted, but the punishments were not appropriate. So I got in trouble at school for pulling a girl's hair. I liked her and she was cute, and I was kind of flirting, I think. But the school called my parents and asked for a meeting to discuss my behavior. My dad was furious and refused the meeting, saying he would handle this one on his own. The next day, a video was posted on social media of me being forced to walk to school with a BULLY sign posted to my chest while following my dad's car on foot. After that incident, I mostly kept to myself, terrified of any further humiliation.

Distortion and Rewriting History

In healthy relationships, people can disagree about how they perceive a particular situation. Differences of opinion are shared, and each person acknowledges that the others don't necessarily share their perspective. What isn't in dispute, however, are the facts concerning the event. For example, if a child falls off his bicycle, a parent and child may have different ideas about why that happened, but the fact remains that the child fell off his bike. In a narcissistic family, however, facts get distorted. And very often narcissists rewrite the facts in order to make themselves feel better.

Frankie, fifty, remembers his father teaching him to ride a horse when he was a child. The horse was a Shetland pony, very spirited and prone to bucking and rearing. Frankie was only seven years old and really wanted to ride like his older siblings. Unfortunately, in one riding session, the horse bucked him off, and Frankie hurt his leg in the fall. Not only did his narcissistic father shame him for being so stupid but ordered him to get back on the horse and "show the horse who's boss." The humiliation intensified when his father told Frankie's older siblings about the accident, and they all made fun of him.

The hurt for Frankie, both physically and emotionally, was so significant that it became a traumatic event to process in therapy all these years later. Before he came to therapy, he had gone to his father as an adult and tried to process this past event with him. Not generally a good idea with a narcissistic parent. His father listened a bit, laughed, and then essentially rewrote history—saying that the event never happened. He added: "Even if it did happen, it taught you a good lesson: to be strong." In fact, the accident didn't teach Frankie that lesson, so his father's assessment was clearly a distortion. But the dad's distorted rewriting of family history allowed him to avoid being accountable for failing to take better care of his young son. The accident, as well as the adult conversation with his father, left Frankie with ongoing confusion, self-doubt, shame, and disappointment.

Another incident involving distortion and the rewriting of family history, which didn't come to light until decades after the event took place, was reported to me by my client Cindy, sixty-five. She got pregnant with her high school boyfriend, and they therefore had little time to plan their wedding. Cindy's narcissistic mother acted as if she was supportive of the couple's wedding plans, but in fact was deeply disappointed that she didn't have time to sew a wedding dress for Cindy—a long-held dream of hers. Although disappointment over her unfulfilled dream of making Cindy's wedding dress is understandable, Cindy's mother couldn't let it go. The wedding dress scenario was all about her, not Cindy.

It was years later when Cindy finally found out about her mother's narcissistic distress. She came home to visit her mom and to retrieve the purchased wedding dress she had worn at her wedding. Cindy had stored the dress in her mother's attic and was hoping to alter it for her own daughter's wedding. When she couldn't find it in the attic and asked her mother where it was, her mother acted surprised and said she had no idea. A few days later, Cindy was talking to her younger sister about the missing wedding dress, and her sister told her that years ago she had worn it in a high school musical. Their mother had given it to her without consulting Cindy. The sister wore the dress in the musical, got drunk after the performance, and tripped on the train, causing her to rip the dress and get it soiled. Their mother simply threw away the ruined dress.

When Cindy confronted her mother about what her sister had told her, her mom rewrote history on the spot, telling her: "It was *you* who got drunk and ruined your damn dress—and then *you* threw it away! I can't believe you don't remember that!" Still upset about her own unfulfilled dream of a homemade wedding dress for her daughter, Cindy's mother resorted to distortion and the rewriting of history, even though she realized at that point that both daughters finally knew the truth. Unable to deal with her own self-absorbed behavior, she had to change the story.

Teri, thirty-eight, a single mother who had to work her way through college and graduate school while raising her children and building her business, also reported that her parent rewrote a key part of her family history. Teri came from a poor family, and her parents were unable to help with her education costs and never showed an interest in her academic pursuits. She became quite successful but will be paying off her student loans for many years to come. After recently receiving a phone call from her father, Teri recounted her hurt and shock regarding his distorted "facts":

My dad called me the other day, and in the midst of a very casual conversation, he told me he was so proud that they had put me through college and paid for my four degrees. I about fell off my chair. My parents paid nothing toward my education and were never even interested in my studies or cared enough to come to graduations. Why would my dad rewrite history like that?

Narcissists are not accountable for their behavior and do not embrace or deal with their feelings. They are usually unhappy, self-loathing people with very fragile egos. Their distortions and rewriting of facts make it easier for them to live with themselves. Sometimes they can convince themselves that their version of family history is the correct one. And they may also try to engage other family members to back up their untruthful versions of a family situation or event. Such deceit is, of course, confusing for those of us courageous enough to stand up for the truth.

Narcissistic Rage and Anger

We all get angry at times, and some of us may even spout off occasionally in a fit of rage or heated anger. We're human and not perfect. Most emotionally healthy people, however, are accountable for this behavior and feel remorse, apologize, and try to make amends. Think of a time you may have lost your temper and then felt bad about it and made every attempt to make the situation better. In doing so, you were acknowledging how your behavior may have affected another person; you were able to put yourself in their shoes and empathize.

Narcissists can't empathize and are unable to tune in emotionally to others. In fact, they often use their anger or rage as a way to control others. When confronted about their behavior, rather than be accountable and apologetic, they get angrier and up the ante until the other person gives up or backs down.

Experiencing someone raging at you can be terrifying, especially if you are a child. But adults, too, feel extremely uncomfortable and disrespected when a person's rage is directed at them. As a therapist, I have seen this narcissistic rage occur in family therapy and couples therapy sessions, and I have heard many childhood stories about parents raging at children. I have also had the experience of a narcissist raging at me during therapy. If I express an opinion that is at odds with a narcissistic client, that client will put me in the category of the "not good enough therapist"!

I remember a session when I was trying to get a father to show empathy and acknowledge the feelings of his two younger children. He got extremely frustrated with me, because he had an authoritarian style of parenting and believed that he should rule with an iron hand and that the children's feelings did not matter. What mattered to him was that they did what he wanted them to do, no questions asked. I was politely trying to teach empathy and role model how to reflect back what he was hearing from the kids and show them he cared about their feelings. I suggested that he say something to his children like "I understand that you enjoy spending time riding your bikes, and I'll allow you to do that after you finish your homework. How does that sound?" He suddenly stood up and grabbed me by the arms and shouted, "Do you know how you are harming my children?" Although stunned, I stayed calm and asked him to remove his hands from my arms and remove himself from my office or I would proceed to call the police. Needless to say, I never saw that family again and still wonder how those adorable children are doing. They are likely well behaved but shut down emotionally, as they were when I saw them. In families like theirs, in which a narcissistic parent overwhelms them with rage, children grow up without a voice. They learn just to be quiet. Never really seen or heard by their parent, they often report in therapy that they felt invisible growing up.

In my practice I frequently hear about a narcissistic parent's rageful outbursts, which often have traumatic repercussions for children and adult children.

Recounting her narcissistic father's ongoing history of angry, out-of-control outbursts, Kisha, twenty-six, told me about one incident among many when she was a child. She and her father were at the grocery store buying a few items when, as Kisha described it, "he totally lost it":

> We were standing in a long line waiting to be checked out. Dad hated standing in lines. I could feel myself getting super-nervous because I knew he was about to explode. Even though I was used to his crap, I couldn't help feeling afraid anyway. All of a sudden, he pushed me out of line and forced me over to the manager's station, where he angrily and loudly demanded that the manager check us out immediately. When the manager told him that he needed to get back in line like everyone else, Dad threw the carton of eggs on the ground, yelling at the top of his lungs at the manager. He pushed me again and stormed out of the store screaming obscenities at customers on the way out. I was so embarrassed—and afraid he'd take it out on me, too. All over a stupid carton of eggs.

Tyrone, thirty-two, grew up with a narcissistic father who, to the outside world at least, would appear to be more charming than Kisha's dad. But at home, Tyrone's dad was a tyrant, demanding that everyone in the family honor and obey him—always. Tyrone explained how deviating even slightly from his father's demands could result in anger and rage:

> In our home, he was a dictator. He had to have things his way and could not stand to be confronted on anything. If I even slightly disagreed with him, he would raise his voice, put up his hand, and shut me down. When his anger was out of control, he would call me or my sister or our mom horrible, disrespectful names. Just speaking up for ourselves was enough to set him off. My mom eventually became so depressed that she had to go on medication.

Dad used her condition as a weapon against her, lashing out at her: "Why are you so weak? Why can't you handle your emotions?" This coming from someone who was never able to handle his own emotions!

Sometimes a parent's narcissistic anger can be expressed in a milder form, but it still impacts the children, whose needs and desires are ignored. Cheryl, forty-three, shared this story about how angry her narcissistic mother became when she wasn't treated as the star on Mother's Day.

On Mother's Day last year, my brothers and I decided to skip the big extended-family celebration and just spend the day with our individual families instead. Mom was used to a big production, with the spotlight focused on her: a Sunday brunch in her honor, a cake with her name on it, and presents from all her kids and grandkids. Instead, we informed her of the change of plans and sent her a beautiful bouquet of flowers with a card and a box of chocolates. She called each one of us to let us know how terribly upset she was, telling me: "I can't believe you would treat me this way, Cheryl!" She gave me and my brothers the cold shoulder and didn't call any of us for three months—until she needed help with her yard.

Cheryl's mother was used to being the "queen" of the family. The kids had learned over the years to orbit around her and constantly give her the admiration she required. When they got older and had their own families, they decided to stop doing this, as they figured out how unhealthy it was. Needless to say, their narcissistic mother did not approve of the changes because she was no longer the primary focus. Instead of understanding her adult children's point of view, she was compelled to act out her anger in an attempt to manipulate them.

Moving On . . .

In this chapter, we've looked at various forms of distorted communication in the narcissistic family. The theme in each of these dysfunctional forms is dishonesty. If you grew up in a dishonest family, is it any wonder you learned not to trust people? Is it any wonder you also learned not to trust yourself? Honesty should be the foundation of a healthy family. Children need to know and feel they can lean on and trust the experience, knowledge, and consistent behavior of their parents so they can relax and develop into who they are as human beings.

At this point, you may find that you are feeling some relief as you learn about and come to understand the unhealthy dynamics of distorted communication. You also may be experiencing some painful feelings like anger, sadness, and betrayal.

In Chapter Three we will explore the spoken and unspoken rules that create confusion, trauma, and instability in a family controlled by a parental narcissist. By identifying and understanding those rules, we can begin to make decisions about how we want to make changes in our lives and how we can raise our own children in a healthy environment.

Chapter Three

Spoken and Unspoken Rules

When we were growing up, my brothers and I kind of took it for granted that we were not allowed to show or express our feelings. When we felt sad, we were told to wipe the frowns off our faces. No matter what we were feeling, we had to pretend that everything was just fine. We have so many family photos where us kids have these fake smiles but sad, empty eyes. It hurts so much to look at those pictures.

—Angie, 54

There are spoken and unspoken rules that govern the narcissistic family. Every member of a narcissistic family knows the rules even if they are never openly expressed. Abiding by these demanding directives, the non-narcissistic family members often forgo their own good judgment or their own needs. The net result is that the narcissistic family code stifles individual psychological and emotional development.

In Angie's family, one of those rules was to "pretend everything is just fine." By identifying the unhealthy rules in your narcissistic family of origin, you can better understand them and progress toward a more emotionally healthy life. Although each narcissistic family may have their own unique rules, in this chapter we're going to explore four common themes.

1. Don't Show Your True Feelings

If you grew up in a narcissistic family, you probably learned that your feelings don't matter. This rule can pertain to both good and bad feelings. If you are sad or angry, that's too much trouble for your narcissistic parent; and if you are joyful or excited, that's too threatening to them. Remember, the narcissist does not deal well with their own feelings, and—as we discussed in the previous chapter—that's why their feelings often get projected onto the other family members. But by adhering to this rule, and only expressing the emotions of the narcissistic parent, you are prevented from experiencing your own range of emotions and thus existing as a whole person.

Amy, forty-five, shared the following story about her mother's unspoken rule. Her mom would be the one to define and articulate how each member of the family was feeling at any given time:

> *Mom ruled the roost. Dad, my brother, and I were not allowed to stand up to her or counter her if we disagreed about anything. We struggled to keep our feelings in check. I always wondered how my father put up with this. It went to the very end. In his late years, he had major back surgery and was actually dying. We were in the hospital room with him. The doctors came in and asked him how he was feeling. Of course, he felt awful. As soon as he opened his mouth to give an answer, our mother started to answer for him. My dad actually turned to her and told her to shut up! We were all shocked. He finally stood up to her even though it was on his deathbed!*

Jill, sixty-eight, told me she didn't dare frown in her household growing up. She had a narcissistic father whose rule against showing your true feelings was sometimes violently enforced:

> *If Dad walked into the room and I had a frown on my face, he would walk over to me and slap my face and tell me, "Put a smile on that pretty little face!" Then he would rail on about all the things I should be grateful for and tell me how selfish I was.*

This violent response from Jill's father tells us that he feels he is being threatened. He personalizes that his daughter's frown indicates a weakness in his parenting, rather than realizing that it is perfectly normal to have various feelings about what is going on in our lives. Telling his daughter that she is selfish for being sad is a projection of his own selfishness and is a common theme among parental narcissists. Such distorted criticism is extremely confusing to a child and can't help but have repercussions for an adult child of a narcissistic parent.

In therapy for the first time, Craig, forty-four, wanted to heal from the fallout of growing up in a narcissistic family. He reported that his mother was the narcissist and that she was the only person in the family allowed to express feelings. Having suppressed his own feelings for so long, as an adult Craig couldn't actually identify what he was feeling. He would say he felt bad or uncomfortable, but he was unable to call specific feelings to the surface. We spent several weeks of therapy helping him to identify any feelings he had. When I would validate those feelings for him, Craig was elated. He kept saying, "I finally feel seen and heard, and I can now see and hear myself, too." Craig's initial response when we started this process was to apologize to me for feeling sad or angry or scared. It was a relief for him to find out that his feelings were normal and okay to have.

Even feelings of excitement or joyfulness can be forbidden in narcissistic families. Why wouldn't it be okay to express positive feelings? Because if the narcissistic parent isn't feeling joyful or excited, a son or daughter's feelings of pleasure make the parent feel inferior and uncomfortable. It means the child is breaking the rules by outshining the parent—simply by expressing feelings of happiness.

Elizabeth, thirty-two, was proud and excited about getting her master's degree in journalism. She had high hopes of becoming a journalist for a television network. Her parents attended her graduation and had a small backyard party for her with *their* friends, but deep down her mother could not tolerate Elizabeth's excitement and pride in her accomplishment. Elizabeth told me:

> *At first, I was just thrilled that my parents were appreciating my hard work, attending my graduation, and offering to have a party in my honor. I soon realized, though, that* my friends *were not invited to the party, and the people that did come were my parents' friends. It dawned on me that it was their bragging-rights party. It reflected well on them that I had done so well. What made things worse was that right before the guests arrived, my mother told me, "Now, Beth, don't talk that much about yourself or your degree or plans for a career. It will come across as boastful and it will embarrass*

me." My heart sank and I thought: What was the purpose of the party if not to celebrate me *for a change? I remember only staying at the party for a short time and then going out with my friends. My one day to celebrate my achievement was ruined. I wanted my parents to be happy for me and to allow me my happiness. But I was sad on the day that I should have been joyful and proud.*

Elizabeth's narcissistic mother was far too threatened and jealous of Elizabeth to allow her to express her joyful feeling of accomplishment. Although Elizabeth's mother had an associate degree, the fact that her daughter was receiving a master's degree left her feeling insecure and inadequate. Even more difficult for this narcissistic parent was the fact that Elizabeth was so happy. So Elizabeth's mother had to enforce her "rule": don't embarrass me by showing off and acting too happy.

2. Keep Up the "Perfect Family" Image

In the narcissistic family, how you look to the outside world is more important than who you are or how you feel. Everyone in the family is aware of the importance of keeping up the "perfect family" image, so each member must demonstrate to those outside the family that "everything is fine" all the time. We all know that there is no such thing as a perfect family, perfect parents, or a perfect life. Life has challenges and people have challenges. In fact, do you know anyone who isn't struggling with something in their lives? It's all a part of the ebb and flow of the human journey. But if the family is led by a narcissistic parent, putting on a good show is a prominent rule. This appearance of perfection serves as a cover-up for the narcissist's deficiencies. And as you can imagine or have experienced, it is not only exhausting to constantly put on this show, but it also prevents authenticity.

Fiona, thirty-seven, shares this story about her narcissistic mother's need to present a perfect image for visitors to their home:

My mother was not really a good housekeeper and didn't seem to care that much if things got messy at home, but if someone was coming to visit, like

family or friends, we had to make sure the house was perfect. We were sent
to the bathrooms with toothbrushes to make sure we got the grout clean, and
we all had to work until the house was to Mom's satisfaction before anyone
showed up for a visit. Heaven forbid if even one window was not sparkly
clean. It actually made us dread having company, and none of us felt com-
fortable with this need to have a perfect-looking house. As an adult, I do like
a clean and orderly house, but if a friend came by and things weren't perfect,
I would be fine with that. But it's like the perfect house was my mom's ego.

One of the traits of narcissistic personality disorder is being preoccupied with fantasies of unlimited success and power, so presenting the
perfect house can be a part of that. Requiring excessive admiration and
exploiting others to meet one's own needs are also associated with the
disorder.

Derek, forty-eight, seemed to be in constant battle with his narcissistic
father, who nonetheless insisted that Derek not talk about their fights
with anyone else, in order to present the image of a happy family:

My dad was pretty mean and abusive and would say awful things to me.
I could never please him. But if I was upset from one of these fights, and
going out with friends, he gave me the clear message to buck up and not
let anyone know that we'd had a fight. I guess he thought our fights would
make him look bad. We learned to both be in denial and keep secrets about
the dysfunctional family we lived in.

Derek's father did not want his son telling the real truth about how
mean he was. The facts concerning their private interactions were to be
kept behind closed doors. When they were in public, Derek was treated
nicely. It was all about making certain that the father looked good.

Joni, thirty-four, tells a common story about the difference between
social media postings and reality. In this case, her narcissistic mother's
self-centered arguments during holiday meals are invisible in the smiling
photos for public display:

I hate Facebook! I have to stay away from it. Whether it's a special occasion
or a holiday, we can have a huge fight in our family, usually started by my

*mother, and then a few days later, she'll post all these pictures on Facebook
of us gathered around the holiday table like we are this big happy family. It
disgusts me.*

Joni's complaint is one I hear from a number of my clients. The image
of their "perfect happy family" is proudly presented in photos on social
media, when in fact the people in those pictures are far from happy. Such
flaunting of an untruthful image is necessary for the narcissistic parent to
assure herself that the way she behaves toward her family has no negative
repercussions and that everything is just fine.

Austin and Andrea, twenty-eight-year-old twins, were in therapy to
process their upbringing together. During the COVID-19 pandemic, a
strange thing happened one day on our Zoom call. The sister and brother
usually looked healthy and strong, but during this session they both
looked exhausted and pale. I knew something was up, so I asked them if
they were okay. They looked at each other with questioning expressions
and then reported this:

*We know this is stupid, but we both have COVID, and our parents have told
us to stay home but not to tell anyone! Our mom thinks that because we got
COVID while living at home during the pandemic, it makes her look bad
and that our family was not careful enough. We don't dare tell any extended
family members either. We're sure our grandma, who is narcissistic like
Mom is, would just blame us all rather than feel bad for us and help us. It's
a relief to finally tell someone.*

In this case, even getting sick is against a narcissistic parent's rules,
because illness doesn't present an image of perfection and is therefore an
uncomfortable burden for the parent.

Narcissists like to win and be the best. They want to present themselves
and their families as better than others. While there's nothing wrong with
trying to be the best you can be in life, there is something wrong with not
being authentic and forcing others in the family to uphold this level of
perfectionism just so the narcissist can feel good. The narcissist demands
automatic compliance and is usually unaware of how this impacts others. This is another example of lack of empathy.

3. Parental Needs Take Precedence Over Children's Needs

In a healthy family, there is a clear hierarchy. The parents are there to take care of the children, not the other way around. In the narcissistic family, it's all about the parental narcissist's needs. Approval of the children is based on their meeting the parent's needs. As author Nanette Gartrell, M.D., puts it, "Narcissistic parents are always there *when they need you!*"[3]

Stephanie, fifty-nine, reports that in her family of origin, her father's needs always came first:

I remember in high school, I wanted so badly to be on the swim team. I had been swimming for years and felt I had a good chance to be on the varsity swim team. Being on the team involved a lot of practices and swim meets in the summer— and you had to attend all of them. Dad insisted, however, that my mom and I accompany him on a business trip so that he could make a good impression on a potential new client. They could have gone without me while I stayed with a girlfriend's family and kept up with my swimming, but Dad wouldn't hear of it. He told me, "Your being on some high school swim team isn't a big deal. Being there for your dad is. End of discussion." I knew better than to argue with him. Whatever he decided was the way it was going to be. The fact that what mattered most to me at that age was being on the swim team didn't matter at all to him.

The inability of Stephanie's father to support his daughter's interest in competitive swimming and the next story about a father's failure to look more deeply into his son's academic difficulties have their root in the same problem: narcissistic parents putting their own needs ahead of their child's. In a healthy parenting environment, a child's needs are acknowledged with an openness to fulfilling them. For example, if a child is not doing well in school, the parent will want to investigate what the problem is, where the child needs help, and how to support the child.

As Ivan, fifty, reported to me about his early family experiences, receiving bad grades inspired a very different response:

I'm convinced my dad was a narcissist. Everything was about him, even my report cards. I didn't do that well in junior high, and one day I remember

bringing home my first grade of F. Instead of helping me, getting me a tutor
or something like that, I had deeply embarrassed my father and there was hell
to pay. I was now a burden to him. His main reaction was to call me lazy,
disobedient, and "just looking for attention." I actually liked school; I just
needed some help with my math, but helping me was not a priority for him.

Clearly, name-calling and punishment are not the way to attend to a
child's need for academic improvement. But Ivan's dad could only consider his son's bad grades in terms of how they reflected poorly on him.
So lashing out in anger took the place of doing the right thing and helping his son.

Sometimes a narcissistic parent who puts their own needs first will
rely on their child to fill in for them in an inappropriate way. This was the
case in Bonnie's early life. Bonnie's mother had a history of anxiety and
depression, but rather than confront these conditions by reaching out to a
counselor or therapist, she relied on her daughter to maintain the family
image.

When Bonnie, fifty-four, started processing her relationship to her
mother in therapy, she told me:

I didn't get to have a normal childhood. It was like I was always the hidden
hostess for my mom. If she was having women friends over for lunch or some
charity meeting or to play cards, I'd be the one to make the lunch, serve it,
and clean up afterward. Mom couldn't handle it but instilled in me that it
was important to make sure her company felt welcome. She never expressed
any concern that there might have been something I would have wanted to
do instead—like be with my friends. And I didn't feel confident enough to
go against her. I guess I bought into her notion that being a good daughter
meant seeing to your parent's needs first before my own. I'm angry about
that now, but at the time, I just did it.

Each of these stories exemplifies a child's fundamental needs not
being met. Sadly, in such cases children learn early on that they are there
to serve their parent. The parent's needs become a moving target that
the child attempts to keep meeting. But because that target is often un-

predictable, fulfilling the parent's needs becomes impossible, causing the child to feel like a failure. This is one more reason why those internalized messages of "not being good enough" get so ingrained in adult children of narcissistic parents.

4. Children Are Not Entitled to Boundaries or Privacy

In the narcissistic family, there is typically a lack of boundaries with respect to interpersonal relationships and private space. The children are seen more as objects than people with their own needs. And it is the narcissistic parent, with their needs always of uppermost importance, who determines whatever limited boundaries exist.

We all have a healthy need to have boundaries around our physical space, emotional space, and our belongings. Think about how you function in your home right now. You may or may not live with other people, but if you do, you can clearly identify what is yours. These are your clothes, your books, your products, your bed, and even sometimes your chair. We also have boundaries around our bodies. We get to decide who touches us and when, and how close others can be to our face when talking to us. We also have private thoughts and private writings, such as our texts, emails, and journals. If you grow up in a narcissistic family, these kinds of boundaries are not respected and are often overrun by the narcissist, particularly if it serves their purpose.

A number of clients I have worked with over the years have been sexually abused by a narcissistic parent. The extreme lack of boundaries is clearly obvious when it comes to sexual abuse of any kind. The needs of the sex offender take precedence over those of their victim, with a complete lack of empathy for the victim. In other words, the victim—even if they are the sex offender's own child—is objectified and exploited for the gratification of the offender. Many of my sexual abuse clients report that their abuser didn't say anything before or during the abuse and that they, the victim, froze or dissociated while being abused. Other clients have told me that the narcissist manipulated them by rationalizing the sexual abuse. For example, a classic excuse is that the abuser tells his daughter that he wants to teach her about how to make a man happy so that she can have good relationships in the future. Sadly, victims of incest often blame themselves for the shame they feel. There are many books and treatment programs written for victims of sexual abuse, and you will find a number of these listed in the Suggested Reading section at the end of the book.

But narcissistic parents may breach other essential boundaries as well. Jim, fifty-five, told me that he had no privacy in the bathroom when he was growing up—even when he was a teenager. Both of his parents would walk in and out of the bathroom as they pleased while Jim was bathing or showering and even while using the toilet. There was no lock on the bathroom door. When he finally spoke up and asked that a lock be installed, his parents teased him about being "uptight." Clearly, as long as they felt comfortable, Jim's parents cared little for how their boundary-less protocol affected their son.

Monique, forty-six, has a similar story concerning a lack of boundaries and privacy. As long as her narcissistic mother was comfortable, nothing else mattered:

We lived in a small house and my mom kept some of her clothes in my small closet. I didn't mind sharing a closet with her, but whenever she needed to get something out of the closet, she'd just walk right in, without knocking, and leave my door wide open. Sometimes I'd be getting dressed or in my underwear, and my brothers or father might see me. When I said something to her about knocking first, Mom just made fun of me for being too shy and secretive, saying, "It's no big deal, Monique!" But it was a big deal to me. I had to go along with her way of doing things—and my lack of privacy.

Taking away a child's privacy is sometimes used as a punishment, as many of my clients have reported. Their parents would remove their bedroom doors in order to punish them for wrongdoing, leaving the child with no place to dress or sleep in private.

A narcissistic parent's inability to consider their child as a separate individual often translates into their unwillingness to allow the child to have their own space—and their own thoughts. The parent feels that they have the right to know everything about what the child is doing and thinking, because they believe the child is an extension of themselves.

Trisha, sixty-six, told me about her lack of privacy when it came to her journals:

I used to love to write in diaries when I was growing up. It was my special time to process my feelings and the things that were happening in my world. One day, I came home from school and discovered that my mother had found five diaries from a hidden place in my room and not only was reading them but was copying down some of the things I said in them. I felt so violated, but when I confronted her, she told me, "You're my daughter, and I'm entitled to know what's going on with you." After that, I never kept a journal anymore.

Thoughts written down in a diary are not all that a child might want to keep private, or at least limited to a few close confidants. Larry learned early on not to share personal information with his mother. He told me that his mom felt it was her prerogative to pass on whatever he told her about his personal life to other extended family members. This left Larry feeling that there was no respect for his privacy. He felt terribly betrayed and told me:

I might share something about my day at school or what my girlfriend told me and before I knew it, the whole family knew everything I had shared with my mom. My mother would listen as if the conversation was just for the two of us, but pretty soon everyone knew what I had told her in private. I learned not to share anything that I didn't want to spread through the whole family.

The lack of boundaries can extend to a child's possessions as well. Once she became a teenager, Ciara was obliged to share her jewelry with her narcissistic mother. Without asking, her mom simply took it for granted that what was Ciara's was also hers. Now forty-three, Ciara told me:

When I got old enough to make my own money, I loved to buy fashionable earrings and bracelets. Unfortunately, Mom's taste was similar to mine, so even though I bought them myself, Mom would just help herself to my new earrings whenever she felt like it. I would go to get them out of my jewelry box and find they were gone. Sure enough, I would find them in Mom's drawer or on her bureau . . . or she'd be wearing them. She never felt she needed to ask me first. When I said something about earning the money to buy the earrings, she told me that if it weren't for her putting in a good word for me, I would never have gotten the after-school job.

Depriving a child of their own beliefs can also be a form of parental narcissism. When a parent insists their belief takes precedence over anything a child may grow to believe, they annihilate the child's ability to think, ponder, and discover answers on their own. Carol, fifty-five, said that in her family "you didn't have a right to your own beliefs about anything":

My parents were very authoritarian and were staunch Catholics. They also had strong political views. There were no boundaries in the family about belief systems. You had to believe as they did, or you were shamed and humiliated and lectured. Being told you were wrong, and you would probably go to hell, did not feel safe to me, so I learned not to express anything different from them. It took me a long time in adulthood to form my own belief system about many things while working my recovery.

Sadly, even the thoughts in your head are not your own in a narcissistic family. The narcissist thinks they own those, too.

A common theme that runs through the experiences of children compelled to follow these four spoken and unspoken rules in a narcissistic family is that the child often suffers alone. When children grow up being forced to hide their true feelings, keep up the "perfect family" image, accept that a parent's needs come first, and allow their parent to breach physical and mental boundaries, that child is left feeling lonely and confused. Who will she turn to for help in dealing with her conflicting emotions? How will she develop a strong sense of self when her individuality has been discouraged or disrespected by a parent's narcissism?

Moving On...

In this chapter, we've explored some of the unhealthy rules employed in a family dominated by a narcissistic parent. Hiding one's true feelings, promoting a false image of the perfect family, assuring that a parent's needs take precedence over a child's needs, and prohibiting a child from having privacy or healthy boundaries can be psychologically harmful to children, as the case histories in this chapter have revealed.

As we will discuss in Part Three: *Healing and Breaking Free*, it is possible to learn about trust, authenticity, and healthy boundaries and to stop following the unhealthy rules you may have learned in your family of origin, so that recovery becomes your new reality.

In Chapter Four, we'll talk about siblings, and the roles that different family members play within the narcissistic family system.

Chapter Four

Cast of Characters

I've never understood why my siblings and I are not close as adults. I see other families going on vacations together and getting together for parties and holidays. We were taught to be jealous of and competitive with each other and not support-ive and loving. It's a tremendous loss for us all. Even when someone dies in our family, we learn by a text and then grieve alone.

—Dale, 54

Similar to the alcoholic family, the narcissistic family develops roles for its family members, which we can think of like a cast of characters in a play, with the narcissist in the lead role. In order for the narcissist to maintain control and make this dysfunctional system work, the other family members are cast in specific roles that support the lead character.

In most cases, the narcissist's spouse is the enabler, with the children inadvertently taking on the roles of *golden child*, *scapegoat*, and *lost child*. In other words, there is one child who is favored, one who is bullied or picked on more than the others, and one who is basically ignored. Each role serves the needs of the narcissist.

The roles can be switched at different times in the children's lives. For example, the scapegoat may become the golden child at some point, and vice versa. This is all determined by what the parent needs the children to be for them at a particular time. The roles in this dysfunctional family system serve to disrupt true intimacy and bonding, especially among the siblings. And the fallout from this sibling dynamic can create lifelong estrangement from the very people who might be the most supportive—namely, one's sister(s) or brother(s).

As I begin the therapeutic process with my clients, many are initially confused about their role in the family system. Some have a hard time remembering exactly how they interacted with their family because they had to "suck it up" for so long and pretend that everything was just fine. Remember the "keep up the perfect image" rule? As "psychotherapists Stephanie Donaldson-Pressman and Robert Pressman" state in their book, "The narcissistic family often resembles the proverbial shiny red apple with a worm inside: it looks great, until you bite into it and discover the worm. The rest of the apple may be just fine but you've lost your appetite."[4]

While some of the roles in a narcissistic family are similar to those in an alcoholic family, one role is usually *not* found when there is a parental narcissist: the *mascot* or *clown child*. This child's role in an alcoholic family is to relieve tension by making jokes and being funny. I believe the reason we don't see this role being taken on by a child in a narcissistic family is that the narcissist would be too threatened by the attention a humorous child would attract. A child who tried to use humor to lighten the family's mood would likely be shamed and humiliated for getting too much attention and would probably shut down emotionally. In a narcissistic family, only the narcissist is entitled to have any kind of power.

It is also important to note that many people come from an alcoholic *and* narcissistic family. Members of such families thus experience a double whammy of dysfunction, with drugs or alcohol bringing about more chaos and more pronounced traits of narcissism.

As we discuss the roles played by members in a narcissistic family—*enabler*, *golden child*, *scapegoat*, and *lost child*—you may recognize yourself or your siblings in one or more of these roles.

The Enabler

Most often, the enabler in a narcissistic family is the spouse of the narcissist, but a child can be an enabler as well. Although everyone in the narcissistic family finds themselves orbiting around the narcissist, the enabler does it the most. The enabler is there to take care of the narcissist, make excuses for them, and attempt to justify their behavior. They are often known as codependents—people who take care of others to the exclusion of caring for themselves. In narcissistic families, enablers do what it takes to appease the narcissist in order to keep peace in the family. They are typically people who are struggling with their own self-esteem and sense of worth and therefore are more easily influenced by a narcissist to believe that the narcissist is more important than they are. Drawn to the narcissist because they buy into their charm and manipulation, enablers often believe the narcissist's grandiose narrative and think they cannot live without this person. A narcissist would like for you to believe that they are the king or queen of their own imagined empire.

There are also enablers who see through the narcissist and are aware of the narcissist's frailties and weak ego, but they erroneously believe that they might be able to fix or heal the narcissist if they love them enough or try hard enough to please them. Unfortunately, the harder they try, the more discouraged they become, because one can never be loving or understanding or empathic enough to change the behavior of a narcissist. When the narcissistic spouse or parent repeatedly fails to emotionally tune in to others in the family, despite the enabler's efforts, that enabler will end up feeling like a failure—unloved and unappreciated.

I have seen many enablers of narcissists come to the sad conclusion that, while they thought they could help or "fix" their partner and be loved in return, their love was never reciprocated.

Renee, fifty-two, told me how she now views her relationship with her narcissistic ex-husband:

I used to side with my husband when he was overly demanding with our son. He refused to listen to our son's side of the story, and it took me far too long to understand that there was only one side to every story. My husband's. His way was the only way, always. At first, I thought his refusal to empathize was toughening up our kid, making him stronger, so I just kept backing him up and pumping him up even when I knew he was wrong, hoping he would appreciate me in the end. I feel so ashamed and dumb that I didn't see it. I really loved him and actually thought it would all work out in the end. I had some "fixer" story in my head that I would be the one who

would get through to him by being loving and accepting. I now can see that
he is not capable of love.

Brandon, forty-two, revealed how he was captivated by his charming wife and initially showered her with attention and adoration, but she later resented the attention he gave to their baby daughter:

I thought I had met the woman of my dreams. She was beautiful, smart,
engaging, and oh so charming. Everyone who met her loved her, too, in the
beginning. She had this confident way about her and was striking in her
style and fashion. I wanted to take care of her and protect her and have
babies with her! When we were dating and all the attention was on her,
we were fine. We actually had a blast together. But I first knew something
was wrong when we had our first child. All of a sudden, the attention was
focused on the baby and not her. I could see her resentment of the child right
away. The more I attended to my new daughter and gave her my affection,
the more problems we had in our marriage. I could not make sense of it. I
hate saying this, but it was like she was jealous of her own kid! She could
not encourage my relationship with my daughter then or now. It has really
impacted me and my sweet daughter.

These enablers eventually came to see that they had made a mistake getting involved with a narcissist. But there are also enabling spouses who continue to put up with their narcissistic partner regardless of the fallout experienced by their children.

In Connie's case, she and her siblings found themselves outraged at their parents' fiftieth wedding anniversary party. Their enabling mother and narcissistic father put on a good show for the party, but the children knew the truth behind the facade:

My brother called me and suggested we throw a party for our parents on
their anniversary. I was not looking forward to it but went along with the
plan. Mom and Dad had a super-dysfunctional and unhappy marriage
that was filled with fighting and some violence. Mom was constantly trying
to appease Dad during all his domineering outbursts and bullying, but

sometimes she'd break down when she just couldn't take it anymore. The three of us kids learned to put on the show that all was fine, but we all knew it wasn't. So now we had to have a fake celebration? Celebration of what? It was one of the most difficult things I have ever done. Throwing the party, listening to their reflections of fake love, and seeing all those guests buy into our image of the perfect family. I left feeling like such a fraud.

From what Cameron, thirty-seven, reported, it was clear that his father was a narcissist and his mother the enabler:

I knew my dad was jacked up. There was something wrong with him. He was mean, abusive, angry, and never really happy. We could never please him no matter what. But I am so angry at my mother. Why didn't she protect us? It was like she thought what he did was okay and justified it. She never stood up to him or protected us in any way . . . ever. I want to confront her on this, but there is a part of me that feels sorry for her, too. But seriously, if you have one abusive parent and the other doesn't protect . . . doesn't that make them both abusive?

My answer to Cameron would be *yes*. Of course, we cannot allow or condone child abuse ever. It's that simple.

Did one of your parents play the role of enabler by supporting your narcissistic parent? Did this cause you to resent or not trust your enabling parent? Can you understand why an enabler might go along with a narcissist—in order to avoid conflict and power struggles and to keep the chaos in the family at a minimum? Do you have a tendency to take on the role of enabler in your own relationships? Gaining insight into your family's dysfunctional behavior will be helpful as you engage in your recovery.

The Scapegoat

In order to best understand the scapegoat role, we need to remember some of the rules in a narcissistic family. The narcissistic parent is not accountable for their actions, is not in touch with their own feelings and therefore projects those feelings onto others, and is usually envious of others' strength and threatened by the truth.

When the narcissistic parent projects their insecure, self-loathing, and/or self-critical feelings onto family members, the scapegoat child is the one most often victimized in this way. In other words, the scapegoat child becomes the sacrificial lamb of the family and gets dumped on the most. Bullied and put down by the narcissistic parent, and not well liked by their siblings, scapegoat children often feel like the "black sheep" of the family.

The scapegoat may be the rebel in the family, the more critical thinker, the more independent child, or the one who calls out the truth of the narcissist's behavior when they see it happening before their very eyes. The scapegoat is usually the first one to call "bull" on the narcissist's need for control and impossible narrative. Scapegoats are also known to break the narcissistic family rules. For example, a scapegoat child tells her mother, "You say you love me, but you don't act like it" or "We have to pretend everything is fine when Grandma comes, but this family just had World War III here between our very own walls, so how can I act like I have no feelings?"

Sadly, the other members of the family may buy into scapegoating the chosen scapegoat child, thus becoming the narcissist's enablers. So the scapegoat child is not only condemned by the narcissistic parent but by the rest of the family as well. Later in life, siblings may realize that they scapegoated their sister or brother, but at the time they were simply pressured to follow the narcissist's lead.

The scapegoat child often ends up carrying the burden of shame for the whole family, believing that they are the bad child, the bad person. As one client put it, "My sister and my parents told me for so long that everything was my fault, so I guess it just soaked in. I believed them."

Merrilee, thirty-five, was blamed for everything that went wrong in her family, while her idealized, golden child sister always got away with fooling their narcissistic mom. Merrilee told me:

I was scapegoated mostly by my mother, but it was as if my sister, Kat, got the memo. She'd do something naughty and just blame it on me, and Mom always believed her. So I was the one to get in trouble. This happened a lot, but one story that stands out in my memory was when we were in elementary school. Mom picked us up from school and Kat had a bag of candy in the backseat with us. She was secretly eating the candy and then hiding the wrappers under the seat. Mom didn't notice until she later was getting something out of the backseat and found the hidden candy wrappers. She asked us who did that, and Kat immediately said it was me. Although I said no, I did not do that, Mom believed Kat and I was ordered to not only clean up the wrappers, but I had to scour the whole inside of the car. I remember being sad, mad, and confused for being treated this way by both of them. Unfortunately, Kat and I were never able to be close sisters even to this day.

Patrick, forty-five, was scapegoated by his narcissistic father and continues to feel the shame inflicted on him for what was actually a projection of his father's behavior:

Now that I am adult, I see that I was actually a good kid, always trying to make my father proud of me. I tried really hard, but it never worked. If he had a bad day, somehow the whole week became my fault and my problem. It's hard to shake that off. Even as an adult, I still feel like I am carrying this heavy bag of basketballs on my back and each ball is heavy with shame. But it's not even my shame!

Remember the old nursery rhyme about the little girl who had a little curl right in the middle of her forehead: ". . . and when she was good, she was very, very good, and when she was bad, she was horrid"? For the scapegoat child, it would read like this: "There was a little girl who had a little curl right in the middle of her forehead, and when she was good, she was criticized anyway."[5]

The interesting thing about the scapegoat child is that they are usually the healthiest in the family, because they call out the truth earlier than the others. They tend to break the patterns of dysfunction sooner than the other family members and often are the only one in the family who works on ending the legacy of narcissism in their adult lives.

Do you find you were the child in the family most picked on or blamed for family problems? Maybe it still happens now in adulthood, and you are wondering *Why me?* Your recovery work will include not accepting this role anymore and learning to validate and stick up for yourself.

The Golden Child

It might seem that being the golden child would feel great, but this role carries its own distinct difficulties. While the narcissistic parent projects their negative feelings onto the scapegoat child and others in the family, they project their ideal image of themselves onto the golden child. This often results in the golden child's becoming more enmeshed with or engulfed by the narcissist than the other siblings. Given the enmeshed relationship with the parent, the idealized child thus finds it more difficult to pull away and individuate because it would involve giving up the attention and admiration bestowed upon them by the narcissistic parent. Wanting to retain the projected image of being exceptional, the golden child usually has difficulty developing an authentic self.

The golden child is clearly favored, and siblings are often compared to them. For example, a narcissistic parent might say to siblings of the golden child: "Why can't you get good grades like your sister?" or "Your brother already earns his own money; you should ask him what his secret is" or "Your sister and her family follow the Bible and are good Christians, what happened to you?"

Following in the narcissistic parent's footsteps in career or other activities aligns the golden child even more with the narcissist. Narcissists generally get involved with their children only if the child's interests are in line with theirs. If the narcissistic parent is into soccer but not music, they will likely attend a child's soccer games but not their piano recitals. Similarly, the narcissistic parent may provide rides to practices if the sport or activity is something they like.

Golden children tend to report mixed emotions about being treated better than their siblings by their narcissistic parent. Some become smug and entitled and expect preferential treatment outside the family as well. When they get out into the real world, however, they may become confused and upset that those feelings of entitlement work against them, as they are not necessarily as favored as they were in their family of origin. Some become narcissists themselves if they don't understand the dynamics of the narcissistic family and work through their recovery. Others report feeling guilty about having been shown favoritism by their narcissistic parent, knowing that such treatment was unfair. Perhaps one of the most negative effects of having been treated as a golden child is the ongoing need to be perfect in order to keep up the image instilled by the narcissistic parent. Such perfectionism can be a very difficult burden throughout one's life.

The golden child often talks about the impostor syndrome—or feeling like a fraud. Even though they were treated as objects of idealized attention and constantly told how great they were, they know deep down that they are not better than others. This disconnect between how they were treated by their narcissistic parent and what they know to be the truth about themselves can cause self-sabotaging behavior in adult life.

Wesley, fifty-seven, and Kathryn, sixty-six, talked about having been golden children in the eyes of their narcissistic parents. Wesley told me:

I knew I was the apple of my mother's eye. She adored me and thought I could do no wrong, while always finding fault with my siblings. I felt growing up that I would be the most successful of all us kids. Whoa, was I wrong! I have been self-sabotaging with drugs and alcohol my whole life, trying to cover up my weak self-esteem and my lack of success. It makes me really sad now that I'm sober and beginning to understand it all.

Kathryn had this to say:

I knew I was favored compared to my siblings. I had a good work ethic, helped my mom with everything, got good grades, and was involved in all kinds of extracurricular activities that my mother loved. Mom was into music and was a music teacher, and I excelled in music, too. So . . . when I had to tell my parents at age eighteen that I was pregnant, my mother lost it. I had been a virgin until then. Dad seemed to handle it okay, but Mom just put her head in her hands and said, "I would have trusted you on any mountain with any man." That wasn't fun, and she never let me live it down. I had let her down. Her perfect child. She started ranting about what we would tell the family, neighbors, and relatives. It became all about her, of course. Man, if there was ever a time I needed some extra support that was the time.

Of the four children in her family, Annabelle, thirty-one, was the golden child. She spoke a lot in therapy about how hard it was to get out from under the engulfment of her narcissistic father:

It was so confusing because I wanted to please my father and make him proud of me, but I learned that I didn't agree with everything he preached and believed in. I liked his attention, but it was too much for me and I felt I couldn't grow up to be an adult always having to check in with him about everything. It made me still feel like a child. I later realized that Dad didn't even know the real me, he just knew the people-pleasing or should I say dad-pleasing me!

Many golden children report a difficulty with individuation—that is, separating from their family of origin, particularly from the narcissistic parent who smothers them and has defined who they are as individuals. Although it might seem that a child who is treated as a golden child would be very close to their parent, the narcissist doesn't know how to be emotionally close and to tune in to their child. It is like they emotionally suffocate and emotionally distance at the same time.

One can understand the heavy burden carried by the golden child. Their idealized role may look good to the other siblings or to outsiders, but it carries with it an emotional disadvantage that is hard to shake.

Was it clear to you that you were the favored child in the family? You may feel guilty about having unintentionally played this role, but be assured that it was not your fault.

The Lost Child

While I believe all the children in a narcissistic family are victims of emotional neglect, the lost child is neglected in particular and painful ways. Those cast in the lost child role are best described as avoiding conflict at all costs and essentially blending into the woodwork in order not to draw attention—good or bad—to themselves. Withdrawing into themselves, many lost children in a narcissistic family become creative and engage in art, writing, music, or some other inner passion. They report being ignored but also wanting to be invisible, because not being seen or heard from is their defense mechanism, a way to survive the chaos of their narcissistic family.

Landon, forty-two, withdrew from his loudmouthed narcissistic father and focused on creating art. As a child, he spent much of his time alone in his room drawing and painting. Although he became a successful animation artist, his personal history as a lost child coping with parental narcissism took a toll. He told me:

My life is all about my work and art. I have few friends, no girlfriend, a very slow social life, and I am desperately lonely. I do not know how to connect with other people other than through my art. My brother and sister interact with each other, but they mostly fight and cause problems. Mom and Dad are the same with all their glorious dysfunction, and I still just stay out of the way. When they try to triangulate me in the family battles, I remain quiet and just say I don't know. We're a family, but we're not a family. No real emotional connection. I'm used to it, but it feels like a tremendous loss to me.

Since lost children often report being disconnected from their feelings as children, as adults in therapy one of their main challenges is to get in touch with their feelings and really feel them. Because they learned as children to deny their feelings and desires, they have a hard time expressing what they need or want. Learning to do so is a goal—and a challenge.

Paula, fifty-five, describes how it felt to be in the role of lost child:

Growing up, I was invisible in my family. It was like I had no voice. My sister, who was the troublemaker, had a loud voice, and my brother, who was the golden child, had a loud voice. Both of them got a lot of attention in different ways, good and bad. What is so weird to me is that this feeling of being invisible has followed me into my adult life. At work, no one asks for my opinion. In my marriage, my opinion doesn't matter. In my parenting, the kids always go to their dad. When at social gatherings, I am not con-

sulted on what I think about anything. I know it's me and that I was trained this way, but it is so hard to change it and be assertive and speak up when it is important. It's a strange sensation to be in a group of people talking to each other but never to me, and I'm right there. I want to wave my hand sometimes and say, "Hey, I'm here, too!"

Jamie, fifty-five, and her sister, Kim, fifty, are currently taking care of their elderly father. They share caregiving duties, and although they did not get along well during their childhood, they are working hard to cooperate. Growing up, Kim was the golden child and Jamie the lost child. It seems their roles have not changed much in their father's eyes. Jamie described recent interactions between her father and the two sisters:

When we were kids sitting around the dinner table or the TV, our dad would focus all his attention on Kim, asking her what she thought of the team they were following or the show they were watching, and of course Kim always agreed with his take on everything. After all these years, nothing has changed. All the conversation from Dad goes directly to Kim. He looks right past me even if he's talking about something that I did for him on that particular day. He thanks Kim, not me. It is like I am not there! When I speak up and say, "Dad, I did that for you," he says, "Well, let me ask your sister about that." I can't win. I secretly hoped maybe he would notice me because I was helping him so much, but he hasn't changed.

Do you relate to being the lost child and feeling invisible even in adult life? Do you find it hard to find your voice? Lost children have work to do in therapy to overcome their isolation and to learn to be assertive and speak up for themselves. It's tough to unlearn the lesson of withdrawing and remaining invisible. Fortunately, a more empowered life is possible once those who have inhabited the role of lost child find their voice and learn to express themselves.

How Are Sibling Relationships
Affected in a Narcissistic Family?

None of the roles in a narcissistic family are healthy, and each carries its own burdens. The roles we've been describing are not always static; they may be blurred and change over time. Some children of narcissists report that they took on different roles at different periods in their childhood. With that said, each of the roles we've examined causes ongoing psychological issues and usually requires therapy to overcome. We will discuss therapeutic options in Part Three: *Healing and Breaking Free*. But let's take a look at what can happen over time to sibling relationships that took root in a narcissistic family.

Although some sibling rivalry is considered normal in healthy families, in the narcissistic family the rivalry is enhanced and much more damaging. Because the narcissist must always be in control, weakening the ties between other family members is a way to maintain that control. In healthy families, parents want their children to be close and to trust and respect each other. A narcissistic parent, on the other hand, doesn't really care if their children have a close relationship with each other. They just want to make sure that all the loyalty and attention in the family is focused on them.

Children in a narcissistic family system are lucky if they have at least one sibling they are close to—someone who can validate the difficult experience of living in an unhealthy family environment dominated by a narcissist. It is more common, however, that siblings in a narcissistic family are not connected or close, because they are not taught emotional intimacy or how to be in a healthy relationship. Rather, they are pitted against each other through competition and comparison. Since the narcissistic parent requires that all family members focus their attention on them, closeness between siblings is considered a threat. Many adult children from narcissistic families struggle to create a positive relationship with siblings from whom they were estranged, and the challenge can be painful.

There are many reasons for the disconnect between siblings who grew up in a narcissistic family environment. The golden child may continue to be disliked due to the favoritism shown them by the narcissistic parent. The scapegoat child may continue being scapegoated if they persist in telling the truth about the family dynamic and their siblings feel they are threatening the presentable image of their family. And the lost child who felt isolated and invisible may still not know how to connect with their siblings even if they want to. If the narcissistic parent is alive, they may continue to drive a wedge between adult siblings, preventing sisters and brothers from connecting.

Other issues may persist as well. If siblings were taught to be competitive, jealousies may arise with respect to careers, children, money, looks, partners, houses, and more. And if one or more siblings turn out to be narcissists themselves, they may align with the parent in abusing the others.

Jackie, fifty-eight, desperately wanted a relationship with her sister Monica. As children, the sisters were pitted against each other by their enabler mother and narcissistic father. Monica was favored, and Jackie was the scapegoat. Jackie was the oldest, very smart and quite independent. She didn't always follow the rules, but she was successful in whatever she did. This was a threat to the parents and to her younger sister. Jackie was taught to play down her skills because it made Monica feel bad about herself. Also, Jackie had to give in to whatever Monica wanted and was expected to be her helper. The parents' favoring of Monica was habitual, and they never encouraged Jackie to have her own power or voice. As an adult, Jackie wanted to mend this dynamic and try to be close to her sister in a healthy way, but it seemed their previous roles in the family system contributed to Monica's reluctance to connect with her sister. Jackie told me this:

> I kept calling and texting Monica, tried to plan holidays with her and her family, sent gifts all the time for birthdays and holidays, and really wanted that connection. It just didn't work. My sister responded only when it worked for her or she wanted something from me. I had to give up because it was not a reciprocal relationship, and I was always upset by it.

Bobby, forty-two, had been the golden child in the family, and his brother was the scapegoat and truth-teller who had confronted their narcissistic mother on many occasions. When Bobby tried to establish a more brotherly relationship between them, he was met with resentment and bitterness:

I knew my brother was jealous of me—and resented the fact that I didn't stand up for him against our mom when we were kids. Still, as an adult, I kept trying to do and do for him so he would want to be brotherly with me. But he couldn't control the jealousy. When he was at my house, he made nasty comments about me and my wife and children. I would learn through the family grapevine about hurtful things he had said about me. I tried pretty hard to have a relationship with him but finally gave up. Now I'm just angry and sad about it, but I realize I can't solve this one on my own.

Yasmine, fifty-two, also had jealousy issues relating to her brother, Darius, who was and still is their father's golden child. The dad's preference for Darius stemmed from the son's continual bolstering of his narcissistic father's grandiose self-image. Predictably, Darius's preferential status seriously jeopardized his relationship with Yasmine:

As a kid, my brother always got better gifts, new clothes, and more privileges than me. Now as an adult, our father still gives him money and not me. I understand why Dad prefers Darius. Darius encourages Dad's self-centered, larger-than-life personality, and I don't. So Darius will always be the favored one. Now his children are preferred over mine—Dad always makes time for them, showers them with extra gifts and compliments. I may be able to get over how Dad slighted me. But how he's treating my kids is a different story.

Sometimes, children of narcissists are put in charge of the other children. Chloe's story illustrates that dynamic, along with the learned behavior in the narcissistic family system not to get too close to more than one person at a time. Children learn that they are supposed to be the most aligned with their narcissistic parent. They are not encouraged to be close to each other. It's a jealousy thing on the part of the parents. So when children of narcissistic parents become adults, they often engage in a similar dynamic with each other: if you're close to your brother, you can't be close to your sister. Children of narcissists never learn that they can love everybody in the family and that they don't have to take sides.

Chloe, fifty-eight, had always been the caretaker for her younger sister, Emmy, due to their narcissistic parents' neglect. She continued in this caretaking role as an adult when Emmy became engaged in a lot of self-sabotaging with drugs and alcohol and was unable to take care of herself. Emmy forever called on Chloe to rescue her, and Chloe felt sorry for her because their parents had shunned Emmy for never living up to the model behavior expected in the family. Then, somewhat unexpectedly, Emmy shifted her loyalty from Chloe to their brother. Chloe explained:

> *It was like Emmy could only be close to me or our brother, not both of us. So she would align with whoever was giving her what she needed and discard the other. I understood the drama because it had always been that way, but I finally hit my boiling point. I had helped my sister get out of an abusive relationship and helped her move to a new location. I bought her several things to start anew and gave her more money, as I had done a lot in the past. But as soon as she got what she needed, she turned on a dime, because our brother had something new to offer her. She then became abusive to me, and I couldn't handle it anymore. Enough betrayal and horrible behavior. Rather than being the martyr, I just had to let it go, but it still hurts not to have that relationship with her. Now she's stuck to my brother until something goes wrong again. It's so crazy. I don't understand why she can't be close to both of us.*

The reason Emmy can't be close to both siblings is because she learned from her parents that you can only align with one person at a time.

Sadly, many adult siblings from narcissistic families are either not close or have no relationship at all with a sister or brother. Some get together only at weddings, funerals, or other milestone events. And some say they have suffered so much betrayal, lack of trust, and mean behavior on the part of their sibling(s) that they choose to give up on a relationship with that sister or brother in order to live healthy lives with their own families.

The Only Child

Having explored the various roles played by siblings in a narcissistic family, we must also consider the roles an only child takes on. How does the only child deal with the chaos and projected negative feelings of a narcissistic parent? Do the enabler, golden child, scapegoat, and lost child roles apply to an only child?

The only child may be treated as a golden child, scapegoat, or lost child, depending on what is going on with the narcissistic parent at the time; so the role an only child plays can be unpredictable. An only child's parent may project their ideal self onto them, making them the golden child. Or the parent's self-loathing projections can turn the only child into the scapegoat. If the parent ignores their only child, that son or daughter becomes the lost child. Or an only child may become an enabler in order to self-protect against the parent's emotional abuse.

Whatever role the only child fills, they have no one with whom to share the experience of being a child in a narcissistic family. When there are siblings, it's possible that a brother or sister may validate the experiences of dysfunctional family life, but when you are the only child, it is your word against the narcissist's. A narcissistic parent can gaslight you, tell you that you are wrong and crazy, and you have no one to talk to about it. Most only children just internalize that the parent is right and there must be something wrong with them.

The only children of narcissists also report that they don't fit in—in the family or in other settings. Not having had the opportunity to interact with siblings and process the feelings associated with being in a narcissistic family, they may struggle with feelings of loneliness and isolation. On the other hand, sometimes they are fortunate to be able to interact with a special relative like a grandparent, aunt, or uncle who can validate their family experiences.

Marcella, sixty-six, is a successful businesswoman, having made her way in the world despite the challenge of being the only child of a single narcissistic mother. Her therapy work is focused on not only finding herself personally, but dealing with her loneliness and her sense of not fitting in:

I can give myself credit for building my business and for the ability to take care of myself financially, but I have no close friends or groups. It feels like I just don't fit anywhere. I have colleagues, children, grandchildren, clients, but no one I call my best buddy. I guess I just don't know how to do that. It's so lonely. It feels just like when I was a child and had a mother, but not really. She couldn't emotionally tune in to me or show interest in my activities or feelings. Everything was about her, and I think I learned to just not be vulnerable or talk about myself or what was important to me.

Hector, fifty, an only child, struggles with the mixed messages he receives from his enabler mother and narcissistic father:

Some days I am the star of the family and other days my dad is still overly critical and judgmental. Then there are times when both of my parents are so tuned out that they don't even remember what's going on in my life. I've had to realize that whatever I get from them is just their projections of whatever they're feeling or going through—and it really has nothing to do with me. But what kind of connection is that? They don't even know me.

Whatever role or roles one has played in the narcissistic family—as a sibling or as an only child—and whatever sibling relationship issues continue to be problematic, there are therapeutic options, which we'll explore in Part Three: *Healing and Breaking Free.*

Most adult children of narcissistic parents come to therapy to begin to deal with the trauma caused by their parents. They work hard on the 5-step recovery program (included in Part Three), and once they've dealt with issues relating to their parents, many then find themselves working the steps in relation to their siblings. Understanding the dynamics of the narcissistic family system opens the door to greater awareness and eventual healing—and perhaps the chance to improve sibling relationships.

Moving On . . .

As we come to the end of Part One, you have now learned about the dynamics of the narcissistic family system—the rules, the roles, and the distorted communication. We're now ready to move on to Part Two and talk about how growing up in a narcissistic family affected you and your mental health.

I am approaching this book the same way I would approach therapy with a client. First, we have to understand your family history and where you came from; then we look specifically at how that history affected you and your mental health; and finally, we work on your healing journey.

Before we move on, I invite you to answer the following questionnaire, which will clarify some of the issues you may be dealing with.

Are You an Adult Child Raised by a Narcissistic Parent?

Check all those that apply to your relationship with your mother or father.

1. When you discuss your life issues with your parent, do they divert the discussion to talk about themselves?
2. When you discuss your feelings with your parent, do they try to top your feelings with their own?
3. Does your parent act jealous of you?
4. Does your parent lack empathy for your feelings?
5. Does your parent only support those things you do that reflect on them as a "good parent"?
6. Have you consistently felt a lack of emotional closeness with your parent?
7. Have you consistently questioned whether your parent likes you or loves you?
8. Does your parent only do things for you when others can see?
9. When something happens in your life (accident, illness, divorce), does your parent react with how it will affect them, rather than how you feel?
10. Is your parent overly conscious of what others think (neighbors, friends, family, coworkers)?
11. Does your parent deny their own feelings?
12. Does your parent blame things on you or others rather than take responsibility for their own feelings or actions?
13. Is your parent hurt easily and then do they carry a grudge for a long time without resolving the problem?

14. Do you feel that you were a slave to your parent?
15. Do you feel responsible for your parent's mental or physical ailments?
16. Did you have to take care of your parent's mental or physical needs as a child?
17. Do you feel unaccepted by your parent?
18. Do you feel your parent was critical of you?
19. Do you feel helpless in the presence of your parent?
20. Are you shamed often by your parent?
21. Do you feel your parent does not know the real you?
22. Does your parent act as if the world should revolve around them?
23. Do you find it difficult to be a separate person from your parent?
24. Does your parent appear phony to you?
25. Does your parent want to control your choices?
26. Does your parent swing from egotistical to a depressed mood?
27. Did you feel you had to take care of your parent's emotional needs as a child?
28. Do you feel manipulated in the presence of your parent?
29. Do you feel valued by your parent for what you do rather than who you are?
30. Is your parent controlling, and do they act like a victim or martyr?
31. Does your parent make you act different from how you really feel?
32. Does your parent compete with you?
33. Does your parent always have to have things their way?

All of these questions relate to narcissistic traits. The more questions you checked, the more likely your parent has narcissistic traits and this has caused some difficulty for you as a child and as an adult.

We don't have to be defined by our histories. We can overcome a dysfunctional legacy of distorted, tangled love. You may be feeling overwhelmed and worried that it is all too much to tackle, but recovery is worth the hard work, and I am here with you to walk you through the journey toward freedom, self-love, and self-acceptance.

Let's move on.

Part Two

The Impact of
Narcissistic Parenting

*There are wounds that never show on the body
that are deeper and more hurtful than anything that bleeds.*

—Laurell K. Hamilton

The Impact of Narcissistic Parenting

Before the child of a narcissistic parent can begin meaningful recovery, they must fully understand and accept how growing up in a narcissistic family affected their psychological and emotional development. In this section of the book, I will walk you through the essential ways in which you are impacted by growing up in a family led by a narcissist.

Narcissistic personality disorder is often misunderstood when applied to someone who is just boastful, arrogant, and self-centered. While these traits are annoying and not fun to be around, narcissism is a much deeper and more destructive disorder that has devastating effects on the people closest to the narcissist. It is a difficult disorder to treat, and many experts say it is untreatable. The cornerstone of this disorder is lack of empathy and the inability to tune in to the emotional world of others.

The following is a list of the ways in which a child can be affected by parental narcissism. We will be exploring these psychological and emotional effects throughout Part Two. Before you read through the list, remember that these are the common effects reported by children of narcissists, of all ages. You may or may not directly relate to each one of them. I don't want to overwhelm you, so digest the list slowly and just make check marks beside those that apply to you. Keep in mind that recovery work is coming, and there is always hope for understanding and feeling better.

What Are the Effects of Being Raised by a Narcissistic Parent?

1. The child's emotional development will be delayed.
2. The child won't feel heard or seen.
3. The child's feelings and reality will not be acknowledged.
4. The child will be treated more like an accessory to the parent rather than a person.
5. The child will be more valued for what they do (usually for the parent) than for who they are as a person.
6. The child will not learn to identify or trust their own feelings and will grow up with disabling self-doubt.
7. The child will be taught that how it looks is more important than how it feels.
8. The child will be fearful of being real and instead will be taught that image is more important than authenticity.
9. The child will be taught to keep secrets to protect the parent and the family.
10. The child will not be encouraged to develop their own sense of self.
11. The child will feel emotionally empty and unloved.
12. The child will learn not to trust others.
13. The child will feel used and manipulated.
14. The child will be supportive of the parent rather than the other way around.
15. The child will feel criticized and judged, rather than accepted and loved.
16. The child will grow in frustration trying to seek love, approval, and attention to no avail.
17. The child will grow up feeling "not good enough."
18. The child will not have a role model for healthy emotional connections.
19. The child will not learn appropriate boundaries for relationships.
20. The child will not learn healthy self-care but instead will be at risk of becoming codependent (taking care of others to the exclusion of taking care of oneself).

21. The child will have difficulty with the necessary individuation from the parent as the child grows older.
22. The child will be taught to seek external validation versus internal validation.
23. The child will get a mixed and crazy-making message of "Do well to make me proud of you as an extension of me, but don't do too well and outshine me."
24. The child, if outshining the parent, may experience jealousy from the parent.
25. The child will not be taught to give credit to themselves when deserved.
26. The child will ultimately suffer from some level of post-traumatic stress disorder, depression, and/or anxiety in adulthood.
27. The child will grow up believing they are unworthy and unlovable, thinking that "If my parent can't love me, who will?"
28. The child will often be shamed and humiliated by a narcissistic parent and will grow up with low self-esteem.
29. The child often will become either a high achiever or a self-saboteur or both.
30. The child will need trauma recovery and will have to re-parent themselves in adulthood.

Being raised by a narcissistic parent and growing up in what we call the narcissistic family is emotionally and psychologically abusive and causes debilitating, long-lasting effects. Lifestyles will differ, stories will differ, but adult children of narcissistic parents wave the same banner of internal emotional symptoms.

Let's talk more about these effects in Part Two.

Chapter Five

Delayed Emotional Development

I don't understand why I feel this sense of emptiness. I love my job, my husband, and kids . . . but there's something missing and I can't put my finger on it. It feels like I grew and developed but my heart never got filled. It's hard to explain, it's like I have a hole in my heart!

—Carrie, 39

From early infancy, we continue to grow—physically, mentally, and emotionally. Our social, cognitive, and emotional skills are continually developing so that we can become healthy, well-functioning adults. If you are raised in a narcissistic family, however, where understanding emotions and dealing with feelings are never taught, you may grow in all other areas but remain stunted or delayed in terms of your emotional development.

I imagine an emotional vessel inside each of us. As we go through every stage of development—infancy; toddlerhood; elementary, middle, and high school; and even into our early twenties—it is the parent's job to fill this vessel with the appropriate emotional nurturing. If you are raised by a narcissist who doesn't understand or deal well with feelings or doesn't know how to provide empathy, such emotional nurturing will likely not happen. Rather, you'll find yourself growing in all other ways but missing something essential, as Carrie referred to in the quote above. A child may be well fed, well clothed, and succeeding in school—and later in their career—but without emotional support there is often an emptiness at their core.

To an outsider, a parent's lack of empathy can be difficult to understand. How can a parent not emotionally tune in to their own child? A narcissistic parent's inability to emotionally connect with their child is rooted in their inability to be in touch with and manage their own feelings. Instead, they project their negative feelings onto their children.

Sadly, many children of narcissists use their precious emotional energy to try to fill the parent's emotional vessel, which of course is the exact opposite of how healthy parenting works. So while children from healthy families reach their early adulthood feeling nurtured and emotionally fulfilled, children from narcissistic families report feeling an emotional void. This void is very often not understood by the child, who may try to fill it with attention from others in dependent or codependent ways. They may either depend on others too much or take care of others too much, and such dependent or codependent relationships result in unhealthy, unsatisfying connections. Some adult children from narcissistic families become loners in life, staying isolated and unconnected with others.

In order to understand the delayed emotional development that can occur in a child from a narcissistic family, it's important to understand what it means to identify, express, and manage your feelings. Healthy parenting involves supporting this important developmental accomplishment, which a narcissistic parent is unable to do.

Identifying, Expressing, and Managing Feelings

It is a parent's job to help children at each stage of development to identify their feelings, express those feelings properly, and manage them well.

For example, a four-year-old may be angry that their older brother took a toy away from them, so they push or hit him. Until children learn how to handle feelings, they typically act them out. A healthy parent might handle this by first asking the child what is wrong or what they are feeling. If the child can't identify the feeling, the parent may say, "It looks like you are feeling mad at your brother," and ask the child what happened. When the child says, "He took my toy," the parent would acknowledge that feeling and help the child talk about the anger in a calm manner. The healthy parent would empathize with the child, allowing the child to have the feeling and express it. Then it is the parent's job to use the teaching moment to show the child how to discuss feelings without acting them out. The parent might say, "It's okay to have mad feelings, and I can understand why you are mad, but we don't hit or push, we have to talk about our feelings." To a narcissistic parent, the feelings don't matter. The child may be punished or shamed for the behavior but not taught about feelings and how to express or manage them. Elena's story reflects this lack of emotional education.

When Elena was six years old, she and her narcissistic mother were visiting a neighbor. Elena was fascinated with a lovely vase that sat on a nearby table. She went to touch it and was told by her mother—in an angry voice—to sit down, be quiet, and don't touch anything. Elena was upset but obeyed. All the way home in the car, Elena's mother yelled at her—shaming and ridiculing her and telling her what a bad little girl she was. Elena, twenty-seven, now reports having been shaken by that incident so many years ago. She learned to be afraid of her mother's anger and to suppress her own feelings.

This scenario could have been a teaching moment in which Elena's mom could have acknowledged Elena's curiosity and validated her very normal childlike wonder and interest in something pretty—while also calmly explaining why it is impolite to touch things at someone else's house without asking first. The healthy parent might say something like "Yes, that was a very pretty vase, and it would be fun to touch it. I wanted to pick it up, too, and feel that smooth glass. But when we're at someone else's house, we have to ask first. Let's practice how we would ask in a polite way."

A narcissistic parent's inappropriate, self-centered reactions to a child's normal emotions prevent the child from learning how to deal with those feelings in a healthy way. For example, let's say fourteen-year-old Andy wants to go to the mall with his friends, but it's too late at night for his parents to allow that. Andy acts out by running to his room, slamming the door, and yelling that his parents are not being fair to him. His narcissistic father, unable to tolerate any defiant behavior, accuses his son of being "a little hoodlum" who needs to be taught a lesson. Andy is grounded for a month for "talking back."

A healthy parent would have followed Andy to his room and asked him to talk about his feelings, while also acknowledging his being mad and sad that he couldn't be with his friends that night. While a typical narcissistic parent like Andy's would use shaming and punishment without giving the child a voice or teaching him to express himself properly, the healthy parent would encourage discussion of the feelings and empathize with those feelings.

For the narcissist, a child's feelings and behavior are a burden, something they don't want to deal with. Their attitude when confronting a child's difficult behavior is: "I don't care how you feel—just do as I say!"

Melissa, forty-one, told me about how she struggled with depression as a teenager. She had a narcissistic father and an enabling mother, neither of whom she felt she could talk to about how she was feeling. She did have her journal, however, where she wrote about feeling hopeless, suicidal, and not wanting to live anymore. In desperation, Melissa finally shared her writing with her mother, hoping she would be able to get her some help. Instead, her mother told Melissa's father, who immediately went into a rage. Melissa explained:

> *I should have known how he'd react. He had a terrible temper, which my mom would usually try to keep in check, but now he was uncontrollable. He kept yelling at me, telling me I was selfish and spoiled, that I didn't appreciate how good I had it, and that my moodiness was just my way of getting attention. He accused me of making trouble for the whole family by writing in my journal about how screwed up I was. He kept screaming at me, and his final words were "What in the world is wrong with you? After all we do for you, you're unhappy? You're a mental case and should be locked up somewhere!"*

After the journal incident, Melissa was left in even greater despair. Although she didn't try to end her life, she spent the rest of her high school years isolated and unhappy. It is no wonder that kids like Melissa, who find themselves in difficult situations, learn not to reach out to their narcissistic parent but rather to keep their feelings to themselves. Most healthy parents would be horrified by what Melissa was going through and immediately try to talk about her feelings of sadness and hopelessness while also determining what steps could be taken to get their daughter some professional help.

Children experience a range of feelings every day of their lives, and those feelings often need to be validated by a parent. If this doesn't happen, children learn not to trust what they feel. They grow up wondering if it is okay for them to be angry, sad, frustrated, frightened. They may be plagued by ongoing self-doubt centering on such questions as "Do I have a right to feel this way?" "Are my feelings out of line?" "Am I too sensitive?" "Am I imagining things?"

Sunny, thirty-seven, who grew up with a tough, narcissistic father who criticized her for being "too sensitive," talked about doubting herself and her feelings. Her reticence about expressing her feelings is now affecting her relationship with her husband:

> *When my husband and I have an argument, or when I'm feeling sad about something, I tend to hold things in because I'm afraid he won't approve of what I'm feeling. And a lot of times, I don't even know exactly what I'm feeling or why. Or I worry, "Should I really feel this way? Is there something wrong with me?" My dad always yelled at me that I was way too sensitive and to just "buck up." It's true . . . I am sensitive, but I don't always want to have to hide my feelings. I wish I could be more open, especially with my husband.*

Sunny had not been taught that feelings are normal and need to be identified, discussed, and managed. She had to learn how to do this in her adult relationships. Many adult children of narcissists report that they were labeled "too sensitive" by their parents. We can see how the narcissist, who doesn't deal with their own feelings, would think anyone with feelings is being "too sensitive."

Like Sunny, Danisha, sixty-two, learned in her narcissistic family that revealing her feelings could be dangerous, so she became adept at hiding them. As a young adult, she made an interesting decision. In response to a childhood of withholding any emotion for fear she would set off her father's anger, Danisha chose a career that would enable her to express feelings.

When I was young, the few times when I showed any sadness or fear, my dad would come down hard on me with his angry, mean words. Like "Why are you such a scaredy-cat?" when I didn't want to go on the roller coaster, or "Why the hell would you care about a damn mutt?" when my dog died and I couldn't stop crying. So I did my best to keep my feelings under wraps. It got so I pretty much felt numb all the time. At that time, I wasn't sure why I felt this way. I didn't really connect it to the way my father treated me. I was just numb and didn't feel anything. Then, I decided right out of high school to go into acting. I wanted to express feelings even if they were pretend. I just wanted to feel something!

Danisha's experience growing up with a narcissistic parent is a sad commentary on the repercussions of being unable to identify, express, and manage your feelings. Fortunately, her career as an actress led her to wanting to pursue treatment through therapy, and she is now learning to authentically own and express her feelings.

Focused on a Parent's Feelings Rather Than Your Own

As we've discussed, in a narcissistic family, the parents' needs take precedence over the child's needs. Of course, this dynamic is an inversion of how a healthy family behaves. In a narcissistic family, the children are expected to take care of the narcissistic parent emotionally and to constantly tune in to the parent's feelings. Although children of a narcissist aren't shown empathy by their parent, they are nonetheless expected to demonstrate empathy to that parent and to relieve the parent's feelings of insecurity or vulnerability. Since the child's ability to emotionally nurture their parent is minimal, not only because the roles are improperly inverted but because the child has not been nurtured themselves, the unhealthy expectation of being a parent's caretaker leaves such children feeling that they are "never good enough."

Gabriela, fifty-four, had been her narcissistic mother's emotional caretaker as a child. She was so used to taking on this role that she never questioned it:

I felt it was my job to soothe my mother's distress and sadness. I would come home from school and find her on the couch, super-depressed and unhappy.

*She would unleash her negative feelings about what was wrong with her life,
how she had once had such big dreams but nothing was ever turning out as
she had wanted. Of course, she never asked about me or my feelings or what
was going on in my life. Still, I would try to cheer her up and ask what I
could do to help her, but I could never make her happy. Even as an adult,
I feel this pressure to help her feel better about everything. Until recently, I
never thought about my own feelings and what I needed. I never asked for
much because Mom was always so focused on herself.*

Gabriela was so attentive to her mother's moods—and so lacking in
parental acknowledgment of and interest in her own feelings—that she
grew up burying her emotions. Sadly, it wasn't until Gabriela reached
middle age that she began to recognize that her attempt to be a parent to
her parent had stunted her own emotional development.

Andrew, thirty-two, told me of growing up in a family where both
parents were narcissists and everything was always about them. He and
his siblings were taught to simply "be happy," but their parents were
not actually happy people. They were constantly chasing the fantasy of
"the grass is always greener on the other side," which accounted for the
family's many moves. Andrew explained:

*We moved a lot so my parents could chase a different adventure. There were
four of us kids, and we had to constantly adjust to new schools, houses, neigh-
borhoods, and friends. I don't think it ever dawned on them that this was
hard for us. We rolled with it because what were we to do? But I went to thirteen different schools, and I have to admit I didn't learn that much because
it took all my energy to keep adapting and adjusting. If I ever complained,
I was called selfish, and they would lecture me on why I should be happy for
them in whatever new situation they were pursuing. Sometimes, I just needed
to talk about how I felt—with all the changes and what I was going through.
But our family wasn't about that. We all just had to act happy!*

It's interesting that Andrew's parents called him selfish for not being
"happy for *them.*" It seems that their overriding concern was that the
children mirror the parents' emotional state—not exactly a formula for
healthy emotional development. And as far as the kids' obligation to "act

happy," that demand corresponds to a common theme in narcissistic families: *toxic positivity*. If everything appears to be just great, and everyone is acting happy, it makes the parent feel better about themselves. Parents can tell themselves that they are doing a great job of being a parent and lessen the fear that everything is not okay. The toxicity in this charade is that when children in a narcissistic family are compelled to act happy when they're not, they feel inauthentic. And if they communicate their feelings of unhappiness, as Andrew did, there is a price to pay.

Reacting to Triggers

Without appropriate role models for how to handle their feelings, and with the lack of recovery or understanding, adult children raised in narcissistic families may find themselves overreacting to particular situations; being defensive, confused, or overwhelmed; and feeling like they don't know what they feel. Certain interactions with others may be what we call *triggers*, reminding them of something in their childhood, which they are unable to handle as well as they would like.

Let's look at some examples of this triggering effect.

Beatrice, forty-five, reported that in her family she didn't learn how to appropriately deal with feelings that arose in response to her parent's behavior toward her. Before recovery, she would become critical of herself when interactions with friends and others confused and upset her. Triggered because of how she had reacted to her narcissistic father's dictatorial manner, she found herself always taking the blame:

> Anytime I got into a disagreement or argument with a friend or someone in the family, I'd just assume I was wrong and take the blame for everything. Before I began the recovery process, I didn't really know how I should feel when a friend or boyfriend was upset with me, so I doubted myself and never stood up for myself. Although I knew that it couldn't always be my fault, I was the woman of "I'm sorry, I'm sorry" all the time.

Michael, forty-two, tells me that he is too easily persuaded by other people's opinions. We discussed how this behavior can be traced back to having been required to go along with whatever his narcissistic father said or demanded:

> *Most of the time, I don't really know what I think or feel, so when I'm in a conversation with someone, they can easily sway me or manipulate me to agree with whatever they say. In our authoritarian household, you didn't dare have an opinion of your own.*

Anna, twenty-eight, gets triggered by the threat of abandonment. She learned in therapy that this fear originated with her feelings as the child of a narcissistic mother:

> *I have a friend I am close to, but she has two children and I have none. We talk a lot on the phone and hang out when we can. I know logically that with two kids, you can't always be available for friends, but when she says she doesn't have time to talk, I feel like I have a big, angry, illogical reaction. Until I came to therapy and learned about this, I would have some pretty bad behavior. I did this in private, but when my friend couldn't talk and I needed to, I would literally take my hand and knock everything off my bathroom counter with one swipe. I knew it was crazy acting, but I just did not know how to handle my feelings properly yet. My husband would just shake his head in disbelief, and I felt like an idiot. I was acting like such a child emotionally.*

Anna's familiar feelings of emotional abandonment in her childhood were getting triggered by her friend. She learned in treatment that she had to work on her prior trauma with her narcissistic mother to be able to handle these kinds of triggers in more rational ways.

Jordan, forty-eight, is struggling in his love relationship because, as we're beginning to explore in his therapy, at times his partner reminds him of his narcissistic mother. Instead of realizing he is being triggered and hasn't yet learned how to manage those feelings, he becomes defensive:

> *When my partner tries to tell me he's upset with me, I immediately start blaming him. I roll my eyes, act very condescending, and shift the blame. I know it's wrong, but I don't really understand what's happening to me. I just get upset, and it's like my reaction is automatic.*

Simone, fifty-five, always felt alone as a child. She was raised as an only child with two narcissistic parents who did not pay much attention to her. Her primary feelings as a child were those of loneliness and sadness, but she never learned how to cope with these feelings. As an adult, Simone is now triggered when friends or colleagues fail to fulfill her expectations:

When someone denies me something, whether in relationships or at work, I revert to this sad little girl, and I just want to cry. It's like I am acting like a baby who doesn't get her way. I get this sad feeling like no one cares about me. It's usually not true, but it is my reaction, and I am working on this.

The behavior that Beatrice, Michael, Anna, Jordan, and Simone describe is overreaction based on being triggered by past experiences in their narcissistic families. As children, their emotional development had been delayed due to the absence of parental role models and the lack of guidance in understanding and managing their feelings. Fortunately, each of these adult children of narcissistic parents wanted to learn more about their past and to grow as individuals so that they could become accountable for their own behavior and well-being.

You may find yourself thinking about situations in which you overreacted to a friend's, colleague's, or partner's behavior and didn't completely understand why you responded in that way. As you come to realize that such behavior is often triggered by what you experienced in your narcissistic family, you will be less confused by your responses. I encourage you not to despair or give up hope. I frequently explain to my clients that their overreactions are a normal way to respond to having been raised in an abnormal family environment. But the healing can happen.

Delayed Emotional Development
Versus Arrested Emotional Development

In this chapter we've discussed the delayed emotional development that is often caused by a narcissistic parent's inability to teach their child how to identify, express, and manage their emotions, and by the parent's failure to emotionally nurture and offer empathy to the child.

It is important to note that there is a clear distinction between the *delayed emotional development* in children of narcissistic parents and what we call *arrested emotional development* found in people who have a full-blown narcissistic personality disorder. The latter individuals get stuck in an early emotional stage and continue to emotionally act like children, even as grown adults. When this is the case, the condition can be difficult to treat.

Being raised by a narcissist does not mean that you will become a narcissist yourself or that you will have arrested emotional development.

As we will learn in Part Three of this book, we can work on the delay in our emotional development and allow recovery to help with fostering authenticity and becoming our true selves.

Moving On ...

Let's now move on to a discussion of impaired trust, another impact of narcissistic parenting.

Chapter Six

Impaired Trust

*Growing up, I never really felt I could depend on my parents for what you'd call
emotional support. That feeling that other people have—that their mom or dad
is there for them no matter what? I didn't get that. I didn't feel it. It wasn't there.
And there's no way I could have trusted them to hear how I really felt about
anything. Now, as an adult, I still can't really open up with people closest to me,
unfortunately. Even with friends and my girlfriend, I don't feel comfortable being
vulnerable with them, so that gets in the way of real intimacy.*

—Brian, 32

Brian's inability to trust in his adult relationships, and therefore to experience emotional intimacy and allow himself to be vulnerable, can be
traced back to his family of origin. Growing up in a narcissistic family,
the child learns early on that they cannot lean on, depend on, or have
expectations of consistency from their narcissistic parent. In this chapter we'll explore how narcissistic parenting causes impaired trust in the
children.

What Does It Mean to Trust Someone?

It is in the very earliest months of life that a person learns to trust. In a
healthy family, a baby learns that when they cry, a parental figure will
be there to nurture and soothe and take care of them. Every psycholo-

gist is well aware of the importance of early bonding and attachment in childhood and the effects that has on an individual's psychological and emotional development. The ability to trust is key. This trust should normally begin at birth when the newborn is completely dependent on the caretaker for everything. It should continue with consistency throughout the child's life, so that they feel safe and clearly have someone there for them physically and emotionally.

Renowned psychologist Erik Erikson speaks of the importance of trust in many of his writings. In his theory on the *Stages of Psychosocial Development*, he explains why a baby's ability to trust their caregiver to adequately attend to their needs is crucial to the child's development. Erikson's ideas on the importance of developing trust are summarized in an article on verywellmind.com:

> The first stage of Erikson's theory of psychosocial development occurs between birth and 1 year of age and is the most fundamental stage in life. Because an infant is utterly dependent, developing trust is based on the dependability and quality of the child's caregivers.
>
> At this point in development, the child is utterly dependent upon adult caregivers for everything they need to survive including food, love, warmth, safety, and nurturing. If a caregiver fails to provide adequate care and love, the child will come to feel that they cannot trust or depend upon the adults in their life.[6]

Abraham Maslow's Hierarchy of Needs is another frequently referenced psychological theory that highlights the importance of and need for trust. Maslow presents a five-tier model of human needs, usually depicted as a pyramid, ranging from basic needs to psychological needs to self-fulfillment needs. The five essential needs are: physiological, safety, love and belonging, esteem, and self-actualization. Basic needs must be satisfied before individuals can attain the needs that are higher up in the hierarchy. Safety, which includes trust, is shown as the second level on the pyramid and is defined as a basic need.

Practicing as a family therapist for years, I've seen the lack of trust play out with many clients who come from dysfunctional families. I usually do a social history and try to determine where this comes from. Clients will often present with hypervigilance and anxiety issues, without understanding why. When we can trace back to the client not feeling safe at home because of narcissistic parenting, we can begin to work on the problem and develop our plan of recovery. Let's learn more about the importance of trust and how it relates to adult behavior and relationships.

The *Merriam-Webster* dictionary defines trust as "assured reliance on the character, ability, strength, or truth of someone or something." In terms of the relationship between parent and child, children need to be assured of their parent's character, ability, strength, and truthfulness in order to feel safe. And they need to know that their parent will be there for them no matter what.

When a child is raised in a narcissistic family, however, their sense of safety is shaky at best. A narcissistic parent is unpredictable and inconsistent in the way they respond to the child, thereby leaving that child feeling vulnerable and unsafe. Thus, the child's ability to trust that others will consistently see and hear them, and care for them, becomes impaired, and this core of distrust can be difficult to repair. A meme on the internet by "Anonymous" says it well: "Breaking someone's trust is like crumpling up a perfect piece of paper. You can smooth it over, but it's never going to be the same again."

When trust between a child and their narcissistic parent is weakened over time, it is hard to identify exactly how and when that happened, because it was likely the result of an accumulation of successive events. Because a child doesn't understand why their parent is unable or unwilling to attend to their needs, or even if they conjure possible reasons for their parent's inattentive behavior, their ability to develop a sense of trust is profoundly thwarted. If a child cannot rely on their parent to pay attention to their concerns and needs, how can they place their trust in that person—or in others they encounter throughout their life?

Sometimes when a baby is born into a narcissistic family, the narcissist parent finds that the baby fulfills their narcissistic needs. The baby is soft and cuddly and enticing to hold and rock. A new baby may fuel a narcissist's need to be completely adored and totally depended upon. I have seen bonding and attachment begin to happen in those early infant years, but when the baby becomes a problem by crying or fussing too much, the narcissist parent withdraws. Or, when the child starts to form their own personality and starts to say no or be defiant and can no longer be completely controlled by the parent, the parent will change their attending and comforting behavior to that of withholding, complaining, and being irritated with the child, who has now become a burden. Unfortunately, in such circumstances the child may initially learn to trust and then have to unlearn it. One can see how confusing this would be to a young child.

A client who was quoted in Pressman and Pressman's book on narcissism described how she couldn't rely on her narcissistic mother for emotional support, and that holding on to the fleeting feeling of being loved was like "trying to grab smoke." The mother would say the right things, act like she was being a good mom when her daughter was expressing distress, but when the daughter stopped talking, the mother immediately changed the subject and started talking about her own problems. Clearly, the mother could never really tune in to her daughter's feelings or problems. Accustomed to her mother's being all about herself, the client remarked, "I worshiped my mom and I know she loved me, but it was like trying to grab smoke—you see it, but you can't get it into your hand. I still feel that way."[7]

Lacking an Emotional Safety Net

Children who are raised in a narcissistic family grow up without an emotional safety net, meaning that they forever question whether or not their parent will be there to comfort, support, and love them. When narcissistic parents are inconsistent in providing loving assurance that their child can depend on them, that child is left in a state of confusion and anxiety. Children can't help but feel upset and afraid when their reality is that on some days parents seem to be there for them and on other days they're not. If this is the family environment in which a child exists, their ability to trust their parent becomes severely weakened.

Sasha, thirty-seven, told me about the inconsistency in her narcissistic mother's behavior toward her when she was a little girl afraid of the dark:

I remember times when I was around five or six and just wanted my mom to put her arms around me and tell me everything would be okay. I was afraid of the dark and hoped she would comfort me at night so I could fall asleep. But I was always nervous to call out to her or go to her because I never knew how she'd react. It would depend on her mood at the time. Sometimes I'd go into her room and she'd hold me and tell me everything would be okay, and then other times she would tell me I was being a baby and to go back to bed.

Sasha had many stories of her mother's untrustworthiness throughout her childhood. One that she often referred to was about her mother forgetting to pick her up—from soccer practice, school, band lessons, birthday parties, and other activities. Sasha told me:

So many times, I remember sitting on the steps at school just waiting and wondering . . . Will she come get me this time or not? It was scary and embarrassing. Sometimes my teachers had to take me home.

The more this happened to Sasha, the more her inability to trust became ingrained, to the point that she lost the expectation that she would be safe and taken care of.

A narcissist's unpredictability is often reflected in a likeable personality one minute and an angry flare-up the next. Such mood swings usually hinge on whether or not their personal needs are being satisfied. Of course, a child has little control over the narcissistic parent's emotional instability, so the child's lack of trust intensifies.

Anthony, forty-one, talked about how his narcissistic father's unpredictable rage prevented him from feeling safe:

Dad could be a charmer. In fact, friends would tell me they loved his weird sense of humor and how he'd kid around with them. But when friends were not around and something was not going Dad's way, it was a different story. His rage would break out and I never knew what to expect. He'd chase me around the house, or throw me against a wall, or try to hit my mother or sister, or just yell and throw things. It was really scary, especially when I was younger. But the worst part was that we could never tell when it was coming, so it always hit us out of the blue.

Such volatility in a parent's abusive behavior causes the child to be constantly hypervigilant and on guard, waiting for the next shoe to drop and continually struggling with anxiety and fear. One can understand how this would affect a young child and create an ongoing sense of unease and dread. Think about how, even as adults, we need to know that we have an emotional safety net around us with our partners, friends, and families in order to feel a sense of security and comfort.

I Can't Rely on Others

When it comes to trust, the message learned by children of narcissists is this: *I can't rely on others, including those closest to me, so I have to take care of things myself.* How do children handle the burden of this crazy message, given that they are dependent on their parents for almost everything?

As we have discussed, there is a common theme of lying and dishonesty in the narcissistic family, and it plays havoc with the child's sense of reality. The scars that children of narcissists take on are fear of abandonment, betrayal, and manipulation. In other words, an impaired ability to trust. So the child learns they must rely on themselves—even though they have been unable to develop a self, given their lack of nurturing and supportive parenting.

Christy, forty-three, is a case in point. Having experienced throughout her childhood that she couldn't rely on her parents to take care of her—even when it came to providing for her basic needs—she grew up believing that it was up to her to take care of things on her own. On many days in her early years, her parents would leave early in the morning saying they had to go to the store or the fields and that they would be back shortly to be with her and feed her lunch. She even remembers them saying, "You won't be hungry until we get back." Their narcissistic perspective that Christy's needs took a backseat to their own led to the young girl's inability to take them at their word. Christy sadly recalls the following experience that was a recurring event.

We lived on a farm, and my parents were pretty busy, but sometimes I needed food, attention, and just plain love. If they weren't working, they were hanging out with their friends playing poker or drinking. There were days when I was very young—no older than seven—that I was pretty much left to fend for myself. I couldn't even find my parents. I figured out my own plan, which as I think about it now was not safe. My grandmother lived down the road from us and I had a pony. If I was super-lonely or -hungry, I would go out to the pasture and find my horse . . . jump on her bareback and turn her toward Grandma's. I don't know how my horse knew how to get there, and I couldn't find Dad to put a bridle on her, but we always made it. I often think about how unsafe that was because we went the pasture way along a creek. I realize now I had to find my own way to survive because there was no one to rely on.

George, fifty-six, also talked about not trusting that his parents would be there for him and therefore committing to handling things on his own, a commitment that has carried over into his adulthood. George remembers needing help with homework, school supplies, school clothes, and other things, help that parents usually provide. "If you need something, just ask," his parents would tell him; but they rarely, if ever, came through. Like Christy's parents, George's mother and father were untruthful when they promised they would be there for their child. Their narcissistic focus on their own needs over those of their son's led to George's anger, sadness, and bewilderment. He ultimately internalized the message *I'm invisible to them. I'm not worthy of their care or love. I have to figure this out myself.*

George described his lack of trust in his parents and how it led to his becoming a "do-it-yourselfer":

I didn't grow up trusting that I could turn to my parents to help with anything. They were too into themselves and their own lives to pay much attention to me. Now as an adult, I find myself repeating that phrase "If you want it done right, do it yourself." I have a hard time asking anyone to help me, even my wife and kids. I also don't like to hire people, so I'm a do-it-yourselfer on most things. Maybe I just learned some great skills and should be glad, but I run two businesses and am way too busy not to have help. It also makes my wife uncomfortable because it gives her the message that I don't trust her to do things right.

Trusting in a Parent's Character and Emotional Strength

The definition of trust includes the importance of character and strength. How do these characteristics affect our ability to trust someone? A person's character reveals their sense of morality, knowing right from wrong, how they value honesty, and how they behave toward and treat others. When discussing a person's strength, I am referring to emotional strength and the ability to emotionally handle one's own life situations and those of others in a kind, compassionate, fair-minded manner. Strength and character are the backbone of trust. Let's look more closely at these traits and why they are so important in the context of trust.

When we observe a narcissist in their interactions with other people, we see these core behaviors: a lack of empathy, exploitation of others in order to fulfill their own needs, and a grandiose belief that they are always right, which causes them to lack accountability and to maintain a sense of entitlement. Such behavior speaks poorly of a person's character and cannot help but prevent a child from trusting a parent who behaves in this way.

Children learn more from how they see us behaving than from what we tell them. So when children see their parents treating others badly, they are likely to expect that *they* will be treated badly as well. They cannot trust their parent to be kind and caring with them if their mother or father routinely behaves otherwise with nonfamily members. And when parents model a "Do as I say, not as I do" parenting message, children also lose trust. There is a confusion between what a parent tells a child is the right way to behave and what the child witnesses in their parent's behavior.

Ariana, forty-two, told me about her narcissistic mother's rude behavior with restaurant employees and how that affected her and her siblings' perception of their mom's character:

When we were kids, it was always embarrassing to go out to eat in a restaurant with my mother. She treated the waitstaff like they were servants in her personal kingdom. She ordered them around, and was mean and rude—never satisfied with anything. If she ordered something and didn't like it, she demanded to be served something else. But if we complained even in the least, we were told we were being rude and to simply be quiet or we would be sent to the car without dinner. That was super-confusing.

The children in Ariana's family couldn't trust that if they watched how their mother behaved and simply followed her example, they would be doing the right thing. Which is how many children learn. Instead, Ariana and her siblings learned not to trust that how they saw their mom behaving was the example they should follow; they had to figure out how to behave despite the confusing messages they received. Witnessing her mother's weak character—exemplified in how she treated people rudely and unfairly—finally made Ariana realize that she should not trust her as a role model. Like Ariana, many children of narcissists report that what they learned growing up was how they did *not* want to be as adults.

Jacob, fifty, explained how his father's "heartless" treatment of an employee finally convinced him that he could no longer trust in his dad's moral character:

I watched my dad run his tire store growing up. He had about ten employees, but they seemed to quit a lot. As I got older and worked at the store, too, I learned why there was such a problem. Dad just had no empathy for any of them and treated them like they were unimportant. I understood that there were some things a boss just has to do, but when the bookkeeper got cancer, I was shocked at Dad's response. He told me, "How dare she get sick right now when I need her. There's no way I can let her take time off when it's going to hurt my business!" Wow, after that I had to go work somewhere else. I couldn't work for someone—even my dad—who was so heartless.

Being assured of someone's emotional strength is also a necessary component of trust. Most of us would never tell someone about our distress or share our innermost feelings if we felt they were not emotionally strong enough to handle it. We tend to share our deepest or most troubling emotions with sensitive people whom we know we can lean on and who can handle it. Those people have proven to us that they won't be emotionally devastated by our difficulties and will not personalize our issues. On the other hand, we usually choose *not* to lean on those we sense can't handle our problems or emotions.

Given some of the stories I have already shared about narcissists not being able to manage their own feelings, we know they do not possess great emotional strength or maturity.

Yolanda, thirty-three, talks a lot in therapy about how she wished she had a parent who acted like an adult and whom she could turn to when she needed emotional support. Sadly, neither of her narcissistic parents demonstrated the strength required to handle their daughter's upsets or concerns:

Both my parents are like children emotionally. I am there for them, helping them with all kinds of things all the time, including their dumb marriage. But when I need someone, I have to seek out a good friend or my aunt. I would never lean on my weak parents for anything that has to do with my feelings. Even as an adult, I yearn to have that parent I could go to for help with parenting or finances or buying my first house, but it doesn't even cross my mind to ask my parents.

Trusting Others Too Quickly

Some children of narcissists are so desperate for trust and love that they may trust others too quickly and place their trust in people who are not trustworthy. Not having learned good boundaries in their dysfunctional family, they can become vulnerable to mistreatment by those whom they too readily trust. Trusting someone requires common sense and an appropriate degree of caution, which are often lacking in those who are overly eager to forge a connection.

In my long career of working with abused and traumatized children, I have met those on both sides of the trust issue. Some youngsters who barely knew me would run up to me and nearly jump into my arms; others would take a long time in therapy to develop a therapeutic alliance and trusting relationship. I specifically remember a darling six-year-old girl who exhibited both eagerness and reticence when I met her. She had been sexually abused by a narcissistic father and was in foster care at the time. When she entered my office for the first time, she sauntered in acting boldly confident and said, "So, what the fuck do you want from me and where is the alcohol? Let's get going!" Her brash greeting assured her that she would get my attention, but it took her a very long time to develop a true attachment to me and to our joint work together. Needless to say, hers was a very sad story of parental narcissism and abuse resulting in both a severely impaired trust of others and the occasional over-trusting as well.

Nellie, fifty-four, had grown up with a narcissistic mother and had a long trauma history. Unfortunately, she trusted that virtual strangers would hear about her family trauma and provide some kind of empathic response. She had a problem with boundaries and a habit of telling her whole life history to people she had just met. Of course, she never got the response she desired. People rejected her rather quickly because her over-sharing was simply too much for them to handle. Nellie and I had to work hard in therapy to help her refrain from divulging her life story to everyone she encountered and to learn self-care boundaries. Interestingly, while she had found it easy to trust strangers with her family history, Nellie took a long time before she felt comfortable trusting the therapeutic alliance with me.

Blasting out your story to strangers is very different from talking about your trauma in therapy. In therapy, the therapist will slow you down, help you feel the feelings, and teach you how to process the trauma. This requires profound trust and the ability to lean on the therapist for assistance.

When it comes to trusting others too quickly, I've often heard from adult children of narcissists who open up to dating partners far too soon, placing their trust in them without first establishing a reliable relationship. They report going out on a date and telling their whole life story on the first date, which usually results in the prospective partner being overwhelmed and not opting for a second date.

Post-traumatic stress disorder can cause this flood of feelings and the need to tell all the distressing details of one's story to those who have not yet earned one's trust. We will be discussing parental narcissism–related PTSD in Chapter Eight: "Damaged Self-Worth and Complex PTSD."

How Impaired Trust Affects Adult Relationships

For children from a narcissistic family, trust issues can't help but impact their adult relationships. Regardless of the particular dynamic within our family of origin, our relationships with family members tend to dictate how we attach and connect to future partners. Some experts say we are likely to be attracted to the familiar until we engage in our own recovery, which I have certainly seen in my practice and believe to be true.

In their book, *Attached*, psychiatrist and neuroscientist Amir Levine and psychologist Rachel Heller discuss three kinds of attachment in adult relationships:

Anxious Attachment: These are people who are often preoccupied with their relationships and worry about their partner's ability to love them back.

Avoidant Attachment: These are people who equate intimacy with a loss of independence and constantly try to minimize closeness.

Secure Attachment: These are people who feel comfortable with intimacy and are usually warm and loving.[8]

Adult children of narcissistic families often find they have the anxious and avoidant attachment issues to resolve in therapy and in their relationships. Given what we have learned so far, and considering the impaired trust issues we've discussed in this chapter, we find less secure attachments in adult children of narcissists. Thankfully, however, developing a secure attachment in one's adult relationships can be learned and worked on in recovery.

Isha, forty-two, described her anxious attachment when talking about her past love relationship:

I met Jamal when I was fairly secure in life. My career was on a good path and I was becoming financially sound. But the strangest thing happened. As soon as I realized I had fallen in love with him, I became preoccupied with him and the relationship. I couldn't think of anything else and was miserable when he was not around. I would anxiously wait for him to call or come over. I always wondered where he was and what he was doing. I began to worry he was going to break up with me any second. It was like I was losing myself to the point that my own self-care, and even my career, began to suffer.

Isha had come from a narcissistic family with a narcissistic father and enabling mother. It was not until we explored her family history and its impact on her inability to trust that she came to understand the connection between her past and the present anxiety she experienced in her love relationships. Isha's father was an alcoholic and a narcissist, and her mother constantly defended him and his actions. There was a complete lack of consistency in both parents' responses to Isha. Some days the house was calm and the next it was chaos, fighting, and yelling. Isha described this confusing dynamic, familiar to other adult children of narcissists, saying, "One day you get pulled in emotionally with kindness and affection, and the next day you are slapped down again with rejection and humiliation and fear." One can see how this would cause mistrust and an anxious attachment style in Isha's close relationships later in life.

Harold, fifty-five, continues to have difficulty connecting deeply with a partner, a characteristic of the avoidant attachment style:

I have never been married and probably won't be. It feels like I have this fear of intimacy or closeness. I love the chase and excitement of meeting someone new and getting to know them, but when it gets too close, I start pulling away. I wish I knew what to do about it, because as it is, my life does not feel fulfilling.

Harold had learned in his family of origin not to trust anyone and to instead simply focus on taking care of himself. Whenever he had tried to rely on someone else, he found himself deeply disappointed and hurt when they let him down. His avoidant attachment was a defense mechanism learned in childhood to keep him safe from his untrustworthy narcissistic father and mother. Now that he is an adult and doesn't need to defend himself against a narcissistic parent, that defense mechanism is counterproductive. In recovery, he is learning to rely on both himself and others.

Janet, fifty-four, has gone through several failed love relationships, always finding herself too anxious and not feeling safe. Janet had a narcissistic mother who was critical and judgmental, particularly about how Janet looked. Like many narcissistic parents, her mother's likely concern was that Janet's less than picture-perfect appearance reflected poorly on her, as the parent. Her mother focused on Janet's weight, hair, clothes, and even her nose. At eight years old, Janet was put on a diet, and in her teens she was taken to get a nose job. Still, Janet could never please her mother and always felt she was ugly. Her mother even told her she would never meet a partner who would love her. Unfortunately, as most children would in a similar situation, Janet believed what her mother told her about herself, believed she was not pretty enough, thin enough, or good enough. Her negative self-image clearly impacted her future relationships and led to an anxious attachment dynamic.

I never trusted myself to choose the right person, and I never trusted anyone I dated. I was a mess. My therapist told me I had an anxious attachment and worked with me on what had caused it. It seemed to sweep right back to my strained relationship with my narcissistic mother. I also realized that I would tend to choose avoidant-type men, and that seemed to increase my anxious reaction to them. It took me some time to process it all and come to some resolution concerning my relationship to my mom, but therapy helped me. I'm now in a loving, trusting relationship.

Janet learned through her recovery work how to resolve her anxious attachment, find the right kind of people to date, and process the trauma she experienced in her narcissistic family. Learning how to navigate a secure attachment with her new partner has been a deeply gratifying experience for her.

Trusting Oneself

Not only is our ability to trust others impaired by being raised in a narcissistic family, trust of oneself is impaired as well. We've discussed how self-doubt arises when one's feelings are unheard, unacknowledged, and invalidated, and how this void wreaks havoc with one's sense of reality—and sense of self. It's also important to recognize that the key to trusting others is learning to trust ourselves and our own feelings. The more we trust in our ability to handle situations and feelings, the less fearful we become.

When working with clients, I often have them write the word "trust" leaving out the "u." The result: tr-st—you can't have trust without the "u." And you can't trust others without trusting you!

While learning to trust ourselves is a journey, it is a process that's within our control. It is *not* within our control to change those who are untrustworthy, including narcissistic parents. We will further discuss the process of learning to trust ourselves in Part Three: *Healing and Breaking Free*.

Moving On . . .

In the next chapter, we will explore what it means to individuate or separate in a healthy way from your narcissistic parent—and how the process of individuation is thwarted when children are raised in a dysfunctional narcissistic family system.

Chapter Seven

Suppressed Separation-Individuation

I learned early on that I had to keep trying to get approval from my narcissistic mother. I had to like what she liked, be involved in activities she liked, wear clothes she liked, even eat what she liked. I couldn't be my own person. Now I'm a total rebel. But when I'm around family, I always seem to revert back to what they want me to be. I hate that I'm fifty years old and I still care what she thinks of me. I want to be my own authentic self.

—Mary, 50

When we are young children, dependent on our parents to take care of us, we believe that our parents know everything. While this is normal, as we grow and learn more about the world, we should begin to develop our own thoughts, opinions, feelings, desires, and wishes. A healthy goal for parents is to encourage their child to become a separate entity—to develop a sense of self that is uniquely the child's own. The healthy parent encourages this personal development.

In the narcissistic family, however, the rules are different. Like Mary, the child is often taught to shape themselves into the mold of what the parent wants. Sadly, there is considerable aberrant behavior in narcissistic families, so the child grows up thinking such behavior is normal. There is significant pressure on the child to do as the parent says and be what that parent wants them to be. But for a child to grow into a healthy adult, they must psychologically break away from the bonds and rules of the narcissistic family and grow into their own sense of self. Typically, separation-individuation begins in early childhood and is completed by the late twenties, but it's never too late to begin and complete this process.

In this chapter, we'll explore the concept of separation-individuation, why it is so important, and why it is so difficult for children raised in a narcissistic family.

What Is Separation-Individuation?

Psychological literature explains separation-individuation as psychologically separating from one's parents and developing a sense of self. Every person has to undertake this process in order to become an individual. Psychological separation is an internal process and has nothing to do with geographically separating from your family.

According to renowned family therapist Dr. Murray Bowen, an adult can regard themselves to be further along with the separation-individuation process the more they (1) become less emotionally reactive to the family dynamics, (2) become more objective in observing the family dynamics, and (3) become aware of the "myths, images, distortions, and triangles"[9] they had been blind to while growing up. As Bowen states:

> The person who acquires a little ability at becoming an observer and at controlling some of his emotional reactiveness acquires an ability that is useful for life in all kinds of emotional snarls. Most of the time he can live his life, reacting with appropriate and natural emotional responses, but with the knowledge that at any time he can back out of the situation, slow down his reactive-ness, and make observations that help him control himself and the situation.[10]

I often explain separation-individuation to clients in the following way: Imagine you are sitting in a theater watching the characters on stage. The cast of characters are the members of your family of origin. As you sit in the audience, you're able to see from a distance how the characters are playing their roles and embodying the rules of the narcissistic family. But since you are not on the stage, you are no longer in the midst of the drama. You can sit back from a distance and simply observe and understand what is going on in your family, without getting caught up in the messy familial web. As an observer, you are an audience to your family's interactions, and thus your perspective and responses are more objective.

The goal of the separation-individuation process is to develop and maintain your sense of self whether you are with the family or away from them. I call this emotional state "being a part of and apart from at the same time." You can also envision it with the following image: Your family stands in a circle with their arms locked around each other's shoulders. Everyone is leaning on someone. Now imagine everyone bringing their arms down, close to their sides. The family is still in a circle, but each person has an invisible boundary around them and is not enmeshed with another member of the family. Each person is still *a part of but apart from* the family.

When someone is able to accomplish this state of psychological separateness from their narcissistic family, they are free to develop their individuality. In this chapter, we're going to examine various barriers that suppress the process of separation-individuation. In understanding these barriers, you will be prepared to overcome them in Part Three: *Healing and Breaking Free*.

How Ignoring or Engulfing Parental Narcissism Prevents Separation-Individuation

As we've learned, parental narcissism presents itself with either an ignoring or engulfing parent. While you would think these styles of parenting would cause very different outcomes in children, the impact of both styles is the same. Let's look at each of them to understand how it suppresses a child's separation-individuation process.

The Ignoring Narcissistic Parent

If you grew up as the child of an ignoring narcissistic parent, you likely spent your time and emotional energy attempting to gain attention, love, acceptance, and approval from your parent. This then left you with little emotional or psychic energy to give to yourself. You were likely so absorbed in orbiting around your narcissistic parent, trying to get them to notice you and take care of you, that you were prevented from building a sense of self.

Patricia, forty-six, an ignored child in her narcissistic family, is still finding it a challenge to develop as an individual, apart from her parents. She reported this in her therapy:

> *It was hard to be ignored as a child. But even now, as an adult, when I can take care of myself and don't need them anymore for anything, it is still my job to call them. They never call me or check on me or my family. They never ask how I am or how the kids are. They never ask what we're doing or about my job. But if I don't call them often enough, I will surely get a call, usually from my enabler dad. He'll simply say, "We're still alive over here," and then he hangs up. Guilting me but making it clear what my job is.*

Having ignored Patricia as a child, her father is still sending her the message that her life—and the lives of her children—are not important. Her only role as far as he and his wife are concerned is to check up on them. Understandably, it has been very difficult for Patricia to begin to focus her attention on herself and her own development.

Children of ignoring narcissists battle a unique sadness and confusion, wondering if their parents simply did not want or love them enough to take care of them. Without a sense of being even superficially loved by the people who ought to have loved them the most, they are inhibited from taking on the challenge of becoming a psychologically developed individual.

The Engulfing Narcissistic Parent

If you grew up as the child of an engulfing narcissistic parent, your mother or father was constantly telling you what you should think, what you should believe in, and who you should be. They never encouraged you to develop your own uniqueness, so you were inhibited from building a sense of self. Your narcissistic parent controlled your every move.

Whether your parent was an engulfing or ignoring narcissist, the impact was the same. You didn't have the opportunity to grow and become an individual by engaging in the crucial developmental process of separation-individuation, which should normally occur throughout childhood.

In a healthy family, the parent will balance their responses to the child as that child's needs evolve. A healthy parent wants their son or daughter to develop their own individuality and autonomous self. As author Julie L. Hall puts it, "The secure and responsive parent is attentive and flexible, involved and independent, nurturing the child's evolving identity like a growing garden."[11]

Many adult children of narcissistic parents report that their parent ignored them some of the time and engulfed them at other times, creating even more inconsistency and confusion. Most clients know if they were ignored or engulfed or both.

Victor, forty, was aware of the fact that his narcissistic father clearly fit the description of an engulfing parent:

> *I felt like I couldn't breathe as a child. My father was on my every move, thought, or action. It was like I had no me. I was to be a replica of him, and he would actually say things like "We believe this, we think this way, we do things this way"—not leaving any room for my brain to even think about what I wanted to do or believe! I still don't know who I am, at age forty.*

Clara, fifty, whose mother was also an engulfing narcissist, told me how her mom took charge of all decisions, large and small, so that Clara never had the opportunity to exercise her own judgment or act on her own desires. Recalling how her mother was always in control of her decision-making, Clara relayed a particularly telling circumstance: what it was like going out to eat with her family. It seems that her stunted ability to separate psychologically from her mother extended to Clara's inability to decide what she wanted to eat:

> *After the waitress passed out the menus, and I had to make a decision about what I wanted to order, I would always turn to my mom and ask her, "What do I want to eat, Mom? What do I like?" I trusted her to know what I wanted, not me. Even as an adult, I find that I don't make decisions easily. I always seem to ask other people what they think would be the best for me.*

Barriers to Separation-Individuation for Children from a Narcissistic Family

In addition to the engulfing or ignoring characteristics of one's parents, what other dynamics make it difficult to emotionally break away from a narcissistic family? You might think that if you are treated badly as a child, it would be easy to make the break, to psychologically separate from your parents and become your own person; but that's usually not the case. Still, wishing and hoping that things will get better—that your parents will change and become closer to the ideal image you hold in your heart and mind—is a very difficult wish to give up. Many adult children of narcissists keep going back to the empty well, praying it will be different this year, this birthday, this holiday. Everyone wants a wonderful loving family, and it is not easy to accept that our family of origin will never be what we wish for.

Becoming the person we hope to become, however, is possible. So let's look at some of the other psychological barriers to separation-individuation that stand in the way of that positive outcome.

I Want to Be Loved and Accepted

If you grew up with a lack of love, acceptance, and attention, you probably learned to keep trying to get it. You may have told yourself, "Maybe if I just get better grades, or get into a good college, or go along with what Dad wants me to do, he will finally accept me." It's difficult to give up on the very thing you want the most and certainly deserve to have. Every child deserves to have at least one person who is irrationally crazy about them. And that is usually the child's parent, right?

In the course of my research, I have found that many adult children of narcissistic parents become either overachievers or self-saboteurs as a result of feeling essentially unloved. Some are mega-achievers, in an attempt to get the love they need; others just give up and begin to sabotage themselves, knowing their efforts will never help them gain their parent's love. In my first book, I called the achievers the *Mary or Mark Marvels* and those who gave up the *self-saboteurs*. The *Marvels* keep achieving to prove their worthiness, while the *saboteurs* give up, feeling they weren't good enough, so why even try? Both groups are children of narcissists who yearn to be loved and accepted, but whose striving for that love and acceptance thwarts the process of separation-individuation.

Cynthia, forty-two, told me of her ongoing wish that her parents would finally be proud of her many accomplishments and be happy for her. Unfortunately, such improbable hopes tend to stymie our efforts to separate from our narcissistic family. At one point, she told me she wanted her gravestone to read, "She tried, she tried, she tried, she tried, and then she died." Cynthia explained how her efforts to gain her parents' approval never resulted in the love she so desperately sought:

> I tried so hard. I was a good kid, never got in trouble, helped around the house, and never rocked the boat. I kept hanging on to the deep wish that my parents would be proud of me. I got several degrees and have a great career as an engineer. But my accomplishments were met with jealousy from my narcissistic mother and ignored by my enabling father.

Cynthia realized in her therapy that her overachieving was for the wrong purpose. She was still trying to get that parental attention, to no avail. It made it difficult for her to give herself credit and be proud of who she had become in spite of her parents.

Oscar, fifty-five, was a self-saboteur who could never match up to the standard his narcissistic father set for him: *get a steady, high-paying job, like the one I have.* Oscar initially attempted to follow that path but was unsuccessful for a variety of reasons. Realizing he could never fulfill his father's demands, he stopped trying. He told me:

> I gave up a long time ago. I'm on welfare, can't support my family, have a history of drug and alcohol abuse, and sadly don't care anymore. I was a failure in my father's eyes, and now I'm a failure in my own.

Both Cynthia and Oscar, like many adult children of narcissists, are having trouble individuating and separating psychologically from their families of origin—but in different ways. Oscar is still financially dependent on his parents. Cynthia is still climbing the achievement ladder but finds it impossible to be proud of her accomplishments, believing she must continue to achieve more. Both just wanted to be seen, heard, loved, and approved of for who they were as people, not for what they did or did not do. They had extreme reactions, although different, to the lack of love that they needed from their parents. Their attempts to solve the deeper issue kept them from themselves and their own development.

I Want to Fix My Family

The "fix it" trap is a common theme for adult children of narcissists. As mentioned earlier, we learn to be codependent in a narcissistic family because we are trained to be constantly focused on and available to our parents. With that said, many adult children from narcissistic families actually think they can teach their parents how to be better parents. They want to fix the family so everyone can be closer. It's a control issue, the idea being: "If I can fix it, and teach them, I'll feel I have some control over the dysfunction and I won't feel so hopeless." Of course, we can't "therapize" our own families, so this plan does not usually work.

Robin, thirty-six, grew up in a family of domestic violence where her parents were constantly fighting, physically and verbally. For years, she would try to get in the middle of the fights and stop the chaos.

> I used to actually try to stand between them and try to calm them down. It was really scary, but somehow, I thought I could fix it. My dad used to hit my mom and I couldn't stand it. One time, Dad smacked me pretty good, and I ended up with a bloody nose. I learned the hard way, there was no way I could fix this crazy situation myself.

Sean, forty-four, is now a therapist himself. He reports how he tried to "fix" his family but had to give up when his narcissistic father repeatedly responded with words of angry resentment:

> I had fantasies of being a therapist my entire childhood. I was excited to go to college and learn about family therapy, thinking I could maybe do some work with my own parents and siblings. While I love my work and am able

to help others now, my attempt at treating my narcissistic father, enabling mother, and two brothers was a nightmare. It was strange because my dad would call me a lot, asking how to handle my little brothers or his relationship with Mom. Thinking I was doing the right thing, I would tell him what I thought. But I immediately got the blowback. Dad would yell at me, "Don't give me that psychological bullshit, and who do you think you are, anyway?" I learned to just say I didn't know the answers.

I Have to Take Care of Them

Individuation is often suppressed due to the ingrained message that the child is supposed to take care of the parent. Remember, the hierarchy is inverted in a narcissistic family, so the parent's needs take precedence over the child's. The child learns that their job is to be there for the parent. This perspective obviously interferes with the child's or adult child's ability to separate psychologically from the parent.

Annie, fifty, learned growing up that her parents did not manage their finances well. They worked but overspent and often did not pay their bills. As is often the case with narcissistic parents, they seemed more concerned with gratifying their own desires than taking care of their family. Annie always worried that they would not have enough to eat or have money to put gas in the car. She got a job as soon as she could in her teens so she could help with the family income. Even after she left home, she continued to send her parents money to make sure they would be okay.

I was so used to taking care of my parents, I didn't realize until I got married and started my own family that this was not my job. I was working and still sending a lot of money home to Mom and Dad. My husband helped me see that this was clearly wrong and unfair to me and our own family. What is sad is that when I stopped the monthly checks, my parents stopped talking to me completely. I was no longer important.

As we'll discover in more detail later in the book, although we may have grown up focusing on our parents, we can learn to lovingly focus on ourselves . . . for a change.

I Don't Feel Strong Enough to Work on Me

People who grow up in emotionally and psychologically abusive families often feel beat up and emotionally worn down. For example, I hear clients say such things as "There may be no *me* in there, so why bother?" or "I've gotten used to feeling this way. It is what it is." Sadly, it's fairly common for adult children from a narcissistic family to express that they want to work on developing a sense of self, but that they just don't have the emotional strength to do it.

Linda, thirty-nine, came to therapy depressed and exhausted. She grew up with a narcissistic mother and enabling father and had learned it was her job to take care of others, first her parents, then her partner, friends, and even colleagues. When I brought up that she might want to consider taking care of herself, she responded with anger.

> *Are you kidding me? What kind of therapy bull is that? I don't have the strength or time to focus on me, I never have. You're going to give me something more to do? Everyone needs something from me, but I don't have anything left. I barely get through my days as it is.*

Linda was eventually able to see that her depression and exhaustion originated in her narcissistic family, where she was obliged to take care of her parents' needs and had learned that being a caretaker was her role in life. Eventually she learned to take better care of herself. She was an extraordinary and special, loving person, and when she was able to give some of that love to herself, she blossomed.

Needing help, validation, and encouragement in order to work on building a sense of self is to be expected, especially when you've lacked those things in your family of origin. We will work together on this in Part Three: *Healing and Breaking Free.*

The Challenge of Aging Parents

If adult children from a narcissistic family are responsible for taking care of their elderly parents, separation-individuation can be a particular challenge.

Ilena, sixty-two, was an only child with a narcissistic mother and enabling father. After her father died, her mother became even more demanding and tried to rely heavily on Ilena, who was still working full-time. Ilena had been in therapy working on the trauma initiated in her family of origin and had made great strides in recovery. She was learning how to set boundaries and to do only what she could do or wanted to do to help her parents. But when her mother became ill and needed someone to start to make decisions for her, Ilena felt she had an obligation to help. She came to a session exhausted and extremely sad, reporting what was going on with the caretaking of her mother:

> I have always dreaded this day would come. Dad is gone and now I have to take care of her, and I am so tired and not sure I can do it. Having no siblings to help, I am now the power of attorney, need to call and check on her daily, have to figure out her finances, how to pay her bills, and how to get her into a nursing home. I guess this is what is expected in most families, but my mother does not appreciate anything, is demanding and controlling, and criticizes everything I try to do to help her. I feel like a child again being judged and not appreciated. I had gotten to the place where her judgment didn't matter anymore, but now I feel thrown back into it. I cry for days after I go see her. It's like my recovery got stopped in its tracks and I'm emotionally upset all the time. The last time I went to see her she actually said to me that I was mean to her—and selfish! After all I have done for her, that was really hard to take.

Once you're able to go through the process of separation-individuation, caring for your elderly parents becomes easier. That's because you are less reactive and less likely to get pulled into your parents' rules and demands. Caring for an elderly narcissistic parent is, of course, a very personal decision and one that no one else can really advise you how to decide. A therapist may want to see where you are in your recovery process to help you determine what is best for you. I have seen clients who were progressing in recovery but, like Ilena, were triggered into old habits by the demands of caring for an elderly narcissistic parent.

When Inheritance Is an Issue

Many adult children struggle with individuation because they fear the financial consequences, including being removed from their parents' will. This can be a challenging issue for some, especially those who may be depending on an inheritance to support a special-needs child or their children's college education. Separation-individuation can still be accomplished, but concern over one's inheritance may make it more difficult for some.

Danica, forty, wants to have minimal contact with her narcissistic parents and keep her children's contact with their grandparents minimal as well. She reports having a difficult time with this because she is a single parent with a special-needs child.

> My father is deceased, and my mother will have a significant legacy to pass on to her children and grandchildren. I can't work, and have to stay home with my child, and I really do need her help financially now and in the future. I'm always afraid I will make her mad and she will give everything to my sister, who doesn't even need it. She literally calls me three times a day and is driving me crazy. I'm learning about setting boundaries, but it's scary with her, if I don't give her what she needs right then and there.

Danica is in a bind that I have seen many times. Her solution is really her recovery work. She is learning to set good boundaries and also be less emotionally reactive to her mother's demands. She is working on a balance of self-care and minimal contact with her mother. The further she gets in her recovery, the better she is at handling this delicate situation in a calm and sane manner.

I Still Get Triangulated in Conversations

In the narcissistic family, triangulation in conversations is a way of life. You may have done this for so long with members of your family that you don't realize when you've been pulled into a conversation that has nothing to do with you. Your narcissistic mother might be telling you how mad she is at your brother instead of going directly to him to address the problem. Or your enabling father may tell you to keep a secret from your narcissistic mother for fear she will erupt in anger. If family members are still doing this to you, it makes your separation-individuation process more difficult. As we will explore later, you have to learn how to set boundaries and remove yourself from the triangle.

Paul, fifty, is working recovery, but continues to get calls from his mother complaining about his sister. It slows down his individuation work because he keeps getting pulled into the family drama.

I'm not the family therapist here. I try to help and give advice, but then it ruins my day because I ruminate about their problems rather than work on my own life. I want to just say, "Leave me out of it," but I haven't been able to pull this off yet.

Paul is learning how to get himself out of the triangle. The key here is to do it in a kind way and with empathy. For example, he might say to his mother, "Hey, Mom, I know how hard this is for you, and I am sorry you are dealing with it. I'm busy at work and can't really discuss it. I hope you can talk to Sis about it."

I Still Care What My Parents Think of Me

A good sign that you are progressing in the process of separation-individuation is getting to the place emotionally where you no longer care what your parents think of you. You can be yourself, not follow the family rules, and not worry about being judged by your parents. It's important to recognize that caring what your parents think of you is the core barrier to psychologically separating and developing a distinct self.

Mara (forty-two)'s story illustrates how hard it can be for an adult child to no longer depend on what her narcissistic parent thinks of her.

> *After so many years of relying on my mom's opinions before I could feel con-*
> *fident and good about myself—whether it was how well I performed at my*
> *cello recital, getting a responsible job, or approving of a potential boyfriend, I*
> *thought I was getting to a point where I could take it if she made a negative*
> *or mean comment. I was wrong. I told her about my new position at work*
> *because I was really proud of myself, and all she could say was "How long*
> *do you think you'll stick with that dead-end job? When I was your age, I*
> *was already heading up my own business." I feel like I'm back to square*
> *one—devastated by her opinion of me.*

As Mara works her recovery, the demeaning comments from her mother will mean less and less. She will be able to roll her eyes and say to herself, "There she goes again, that's just my mom," but not let it devastate her.

Moving On . . .

In this chapter we've examined the various barriers to separation-individuation, including feeling the need to fix your narcissistic family, becoming the caretaker for your narcissistic parent, and being overly concerned about what your parents think of you. Although the important process of separation-individuation is suppressed in narcissistic families, it can be learned in recovery, even when the barriers we've discussed in this chapter are present.

In the following chapter, we'll explore another impact of narcissistic parenting, which many of my clients are surprised to learn about: complex post-traumatic stress disorder (CPTSD).

Chapter Eight

Damaged Self-Worth and Complex PTSD

I've been to therapy a lot and feel like I've been misdiagnosed over and over. The therapists I've been to tell me I'm just depressed or overly anxious, but I know it's more than that. I can't quite explain it, but what I went through in my crazy family made me feel powerless to take control of my own life. And I still struggle with that feeling, almost like panic attacks sometimes.

—Isabella, 41

As Isabella correctly reports, adult children of narcissists often are misdiagnosed. They usually come to therapy with symptoms of depression or anxiety or with relationship issues. They may be prescribed medications for mood disorders, but their intense trauma histories are not explored or healed. Sometimes this is because the therapist doesn't thoroughly investigate the client's family history or is not trained to identify the kind of childhood trauma that originates in a narcissistic family. And usually the clients themselves don't realize that what they experienced in their family was, in fact, trauma. I repeatedly hear from clients what Isabella reported; they have been to therapy a lot, but the fundamental issue was never dealt with.

So what is going on with clients like Isabella? She spoke of feeling powerless when it came to taking control of her life, and referred to experiencing what felt to her like panic attacks. As we'll learn in this chapter, many adult children who are raised in a narcissistic family may actually be suffering from a type of post-traumatic stress disorder, because what they experienced as children and what they continue to experience as adults is a form of trauma.

The bottom line is this: children of narcissistic parents develop ongoing negative internal messages and thus a damaged sense of self-worth. A personal history of being bombarded with self-negating, internalized messages resulting in an impaired sense of self-worth often contributes to a condition called *complex post-traumatic stress disorder* or CPTSD.

In this chapter we're going to examine damaged self-worth in children who grew up in a narcissistic family and how it can lead to CPTSD.

It's important to recognize that you may find it difficult to believe that what you went through as the child of a narcissist qualifies as "trauma." This may be because there is considerable denial in the narcissistic family system and this causes members to repress or suppress their emotions. There's also a strong cultural message to honor your mother and father and therefore never speak badly of them—or you'll be seen as a bad son or daughter. In other words, speaking about trauma in your family can be considered taboo. Clients often report feeling very guilty when they bring up experiences from their childhood that were not healthy or good, but rather very abusive. Good girls and boys don't hate their parents, right? But we are definitely not talking here about hating anyone. Or blaming anyone. We are simply seeking to understand our family history and where we came from, so that healing can begin.

The Meaning of Self-Worth

Growing up in a narcissistic family, we learn that we are valued for what we do rather than who we are. This message is damaging and has long-lasting effects. The terms "self-esteem" and "self-worth" are often used interchangeably but are actually different. Self-esteem is how we evaluate ourselves in certain things we do. We may have high self-esteem in some areas but lower self-esteem in others. For example, our sense of accomplishment in our career might result in high self-esteem, but how we feel about our looks or our body image may produce lower self-esteem. We all have strengths and weaknesses, and most of us feel positive about ourselves in some respects and not so positive about other parts of ourselves. So our self-esteem may depend on which aspects of ourselves we're evaluating. For instance, Jack may be successful in his sales job and feel proud of his achievements, but he has no sense of rhythm—as his girlfriend often points out—so he feels bad about being a terrible dance partner.

Self-worth, on the other hand, is determined by our internal sense that we are good human beings and deserve to be loved and accepted. Acknowledging our self-worth comes from within and is not determined by what others think of us or by external factors like our accomplishments. Having a solid sense of self-worth means that we know we are valuable as human beings regardless of what we do. We can make mistakes or have failures in life, but with good self-worth, we still feel we are capable of contributing to society and worthy of happiness, fulfillment, and love. We still feel deserving of these things. We see ourselves as a human *being*, not a human *doing*. Our value comes from within—from how we perceive our character in traits such as kindness, compassion, empathy, and our ability to respect others and treat them well.

You may have heard the saying, "God don't make no junk," attributed to the singer and actress Ethel Waters when she said, "I am somebody 'cause God don't make no junk."[12] Whether or not you are religious, you can still believe that although you may sometimes mess up in life, you are still a good and valuable person.

Mark Twain said it well: "A man cannot be comfortable without his own approval."[13] To put it simply, self-worth is self-acceptance regardless of our accomplishments, successes, or failures. While many people struggle with self-esteem issues, children of narcissists are more likely to feel a lack of innate self-worth. This feeling is similar to shame, and it permeates and damages one's overall sense of self.

Internalized Negative Messages

If you grew up never being able to please your parents, you likely received the negative message "I'm not good enough." And if your narcissistic parent couldn't show empathy and provide proper nurturing and parenting, you probably accepted the message "I'm unlovable." Such internalized negative messages can be extremely difficult to erase because they have been imprinted onto your psyche over a long period of time. And even though your adult self knows that those harmful beliefs about yourself are incorrect, your internal child still believes them to be true. So you struggle with an underdeveloped sense of self-worth as you try to understand the disapproving messages sent to you for so many years by your narcissistic parent.

Most people have internal critics who talk to them at times. But adult children of narcissists have internalized negative messages that are shouting at them constantly. The most common internalized messages I hear about from clients are the following:

- I'm not good enough.
- I'm not lovable.
- I can't trust myself or others.
- I'm invisible.
- I'm empty inside.
- I'm a fraud.

Such negative messages adversely impact the self-worth of a child as well as an adult child. In Part Three of this book, *Healing and Breaking Free*, we will learn how to talk back to our internal critics, to undo their negative messages, and to create the messages we want to hear. In this way, we can take back control from our destructive internal critics and begin to heal.

PTSD and CPTSD

PTSD, or post-traumatic stress disorder, is an anxiety disorder resulting from a traumatic injury or experience. The term first appeared in 1980, in the third edition of the *Diagnostic and Statistical Manual of Mental Disorders (DSM-III)*, published by the American Psychiatric Association. It was associated with the combat trauma suffered by Vietnam War veterans. Before that time, the trauma experienced by veterans was often described as "shell shock."

Over the years, the definition of PTSD has expanded to include other kinds of trauma such as rape, car accidents, hurricanes, tornadoes, child abuse, domestic violence, and many other dreadful events. It is usually associated with onetime or limited-duration events that cause significant symptoms of trauma due to exposure to actual or threatened death or serious injury. PTSD causes intrusive memories of the event, distressing dreams or nightmares, flashbacks of the event, and psychological and physiological reactions when exposed to something that resembles the event. A person affected by PTSD may

- avoid stimuli that remind them of the traumatic event
- be unable to remember certain aspects of the event
- exhibit cognitive distortions like blaming themselves
- show diminished interest in activities
- become detached from others
- have an inability to experience positive emotions

Also frequently seen in people suffering from PTSD are two or more of the following behaviors:

- irritable behavior and angry outbursts
- self-destructive behavior
- hypervigilance
- exaggerated startle responses
- problems with concentration
- sleep disturbance

A full explanation of the clinical definition of PTSD can be found in the *Diagnostic and Statistical Manual of Mental Disorders*.[14]

So what about CPTSD or *complex PTSD*? In some cases, a person will experience a chronic trauma that may continue for months, years, or an entire childhood. When the trauma is ongoing over the course of years, as it is in a narcissistic family, the PTSD becomes "complex," which means there are multiple factors involved that must be treated somewhat differently. The term CPTSD was first coined in 1988 by Dr. Judith Herman, professor of psychiatry at Harvard University and renowned traumatic stress studies expert.

Those who suffer from CPTSD struggle with symptoms such as: challenges with emotional regulation; a negative sense of self; difficulty establishing healthy relationships with others; and detachment from one's own belief system; among others.

The following lists help us to distinguish between PTSD and CPTSD. With PTSD, the symptoms usually fall into three categories:

1. Reexperiencing symptoms, such as having flashbacks or nightmares, having powerful memories of the trauma, and even remembering things like sights, smells, or sounds related to the trauma.
2. Feeling on guard, as if there is a threat which causes one to be hypervigilant, easily startled, or nervous and jumpy.
3. Avoiding things that remind one of the trauma.[15]

With CPTSD, there are usually additional symptoms such as:

1. Feeling worthless and blaming oneself for the trauma.
2. More intense emotions getting triggered.
3. Difficulty trusting others, causing relationship difficulties.[16]

According to an article written by WebMD editorial contributors and medically reviewed by Dan Brennan, MD, "risk factors for Complex PTSD include the following kinds of chronic trauma:

♦ Childhood abuse or neglect
♦ Long-standing domestic violence
♦ Trafficked or forced into sex work
♦ Kidnapped, enslaved, or tortured
♦ Incarcerated in a prisoner of war camp
♦ Witness to repeated acts of violence
♦ Multiple traumas
♦ Trauma from an early age

♦ Long-term trauma
♦ Abuse by a close family member or friend
♦ Not having a hope for change when trapped"[17]

Many of the above indicators of CPTSD apply to children of narcissists, namely: childhood abuse or neglect, domestic violence (i.e., witness to acts of domestic violence in the home), multiple traumas, trauma from an early age, long-term trauma (i.e., often lasting an entire childhood), abuse by close family members, and not having hope for change (i.e., being too young to experience hope and feeling trapped within the family system while being dependent on the parents).

The Collapse

When an adult child of narcissistic parents is reminded of a past trauma by a related experience, they can become triggered and may suffer from a CPTSD reaction. I call this reaction a *collapse*. When this happens, it can feel like a momentary regression back to childhood when the trauma was experienced. The old memories make the current situation feel more threatening than it actually is.

The sensation of the collapse can be short-lived or can last for several days, sometimes causing the person to become almost paralyzed emotionally. This kind of breakdown, while frightening, offers an opportunity to begin to better understand the dynamics of CPTSD and to begin to heal once and for all.

Roberta, forty-seven, had a narcissistic father who had few boundaries around physical or emotional spaces. Although he was not sexually abusive, he would make suggestive comments about Roberta's body when she was a child and teen. He also constantly criticized people who had large bottoms or imperfect figures, and Roberta got a lot of criticism from him if she was not in perfect shape. She tells me she never got over the sting of his cruel, critical remarks:

Today, I am married to the best guy, and I love him dearly. He is very affectionate, and I like that. But there are some days he will do things like walk

by me and pat me on the butt, and I have an instant startle response and
wave of anger and want to shout at him. He means no harm, but it reminds
me of my dad, and I begin to think I must not be skinny enough or I don't
look good in these jeans or whatever I am wearing at the time. I know it is
an overreaction, but it feels like a trigger back to childhood.

The ongoing childhood trauma of having been objectified and dis-respected by her narcissistic father is triggered when Roberta's well-meaning, affectionate husband touches her in a certain way. Although she is aware that her intense, startled response—her emotional *collapse*—is an overreaction, the fear and anger from her early traumatic experi-ences with her father are still present. The powerful emotions that don't necessarily fit the situation and the effect on her relationship are exam-ples of her CPTSD. Roberta is aware of her reaction but is unable to reg-ulate the emotions associated with it. In therapy, she also blamed herself and not only felt bad for her husband but felt bad about herself.

Cory, forty, spoke to me about getting triggered by his boss, who re-minds him of his narcissistic mother:

My boss can trigger me in a second. She is just like Mom in that she doesn't
know how to give kind, constructive criticism. I don't mind helpful tips, but
she'll walk up to me and throw papers on my desk, saying things like "What
were you thinking here?" and this week she actually said, "Are you stupid
or what?" These events can ruin a whole week for me, putting me in "I am
worthless" mode. I beat myself up, I ruminate on it, I'm angry for days and
vent to my wife, and sometimes can't even sleep.

Cory's reaction to his boss's demeaning comments might be perceived by some as extreme, but it is characteristic of a traumatic collapse re-sponse. The fact that Cory suffers repercussions for an entire week, ruminates and is angry for days, beats himself up, and experiences sleep-lessness points to an underlying reality, of which he is well aware: grow-ing up in his narcissistic family with a caustic, critical mother continues to haunt him emotionally.

The Domino Effect

I often explain a CPTSD trigger and the collapse that follows using dominos on the table in my office. I stand up several dominos in a row. Then my client and I imagine that the row of dominos is the client's life span so far. Each domino represents a trauma that happened in childhood. Then we discuss the latest trigger that the client has experienced and place a domino at the front of the line. If the traumas represented by the other dominos have not been resolved, then the new trigger can push the whole row down in a huge collapse that feels much greater than the event that recently happened. With this simple demonstration, the client understands how a recent event has forcefully brought back memories of past traumas.

Many adult children of narcissists are aware of the fact that they often experience exaggerated reactions to events in the present; but until they understand that those events trigger a CPTSD response, they don't understand their intense reactions. They often report feeling like they are crazy and are frequently told by others that they are acting crazy.

Marjorie, thirty-two, told me:

I was recently having coffee with a friend and her sister, whom I'd never met. As my friend and I were chatting, the sister barely said a word and was eyeing me strangely. I had no idea what was wrong and wondered if I had said something to offend her. After about ten minutes, the sister got up to leave and I said it was nice to meet her. She responded with "Not sure what my sister sees in you, but hey, enjoy your coffee, you two." I was floored by this insulting comment from someone who didn't even know me. But . . . it still felt like a punch in the gut, and it lasted for days. Why would I let this stranger's inappropriate comment bother me so much?

Marjorie realized in therapy that this incident reminded her of the years with her narcissistic mother, when she had tried to please her, do things the right way, and always be kind and polite, but still got zapped in the end—because she could never be good enough for her mom. The collapse that happened after meeting her friend's sister "gut-punched"

Marjorie back to historical wounds from her childhood, which is why it took her days to recover from a mildly inappropriate comment.

Eldon, forty, repeatedly spoke of feeling like he was a burden to his parents growing up. His narcissistic mother was so focused on herself that every question young Eldon might ask or any need he might have was met with his mother's dismissive annoyance. And his enabling father basically left the parenting up to his wife. When Eldon first came to therapy, he was always apologizing to me for taking up my time, or being too dramatic, or giving me too much information to process. Of course, I would reassure him that this was therapy, and this was my job, and not to worry about me. One day, he came into a session telling me this story:

I feel so stupid. I have been so busy at work, I forgot to fill my car up with gas and ran out of gas on a major highway going to work. I panicked and called my new girlfriend to come help me. I know she would have come if she could, but she was busy getting her kids out the door for school and had to get to work also. She just couldn't, and it was understandable. But I have been apologizing to her for days because I feel like I was being a burden to her by asking her to help. Why can't I let myself off the hook for this? And why do I keep ruminating about asking her for a favor?

We were able to connect the dots for Eldon by pointing out that his feeling of being a burden to his girlfriend threw him back to his childhood and the distressing feeling that he was a constant burden to his parents. His collapse took the form of being unable to stop beating himself up for simply asking his girlfriend for help. Although he knew his girlfriend wasn't upset or bothered by his having asked if she could come pick him up, Eldon was still triggered into a CPTSD response. Understanding what had triggered him, however, helped to relieve him of his guilt and rumination. It took him a while to trust that his new girlfriend wouldn't reject him, like his parents had, if he needed something from her. Even still, Eldon ended the relationship with his girlfriend after a few months because he was constantly apologizing for himself and blaming himself for everything that went wrong. He decided that his intense reactions to triggers from childhood needed to be further resolved in treatment before he would be able to have a healthy relationship with a partner.

Reoccurring Dreams

Although nightmares or terror dreams are often experienced by people with PTSD, I have also noted the presence of reoccurring dreams in clients who have CPTSD. Usually, a reoccurring dream signifies an emotional issue that is not resolved, so the unconscious mind during sleep keeps working on it. It's important to keep track of these reoccurring dreams so the issue can be dealt with in therapy or recovery.

Katie, forty-five, recalls this reoccurring dream that she didn't fully understand until we discussed it in session:

I keep having this dream almost every night where I'm trying to get dressed and ready to go out, but my clothes don't fit or I can't get the right outfit together. Everything is in slow motion, and I keep hearing this voice in the hall outside my bedroom saying, "Let's go, hurry up, it's time to leave!" But I just can't get it together fast enough, no matter how I try.

When Katie and I first discussed her dream, she wondered if maybe the voice in the hall telling her to hurry was that of her husband, bugging her to get ready, as he sometimes did in real life. But then she relayed something significant about how she felt in the dream. She said that there was a part of her that didn't want to go along with what the voice was telling her to do. She was actually kind of enjoying the slow motion. So maybe she wanted things to slow down, to ignore the voice, and not wear the clothes she was trying on? When I suggested that possibility, she smiled. And then she said this:

Maybe the voice in the hall was actually my authentic self, telling me to come as you are . . . that you're good enough just the way you are. Maybe it was my "not good enough" issue trying to get processed.

A significant part of Katie's family-of-origin trauma was the message she got from her narcissistic parents that it was not okay to be your authentic self. The message was clearly relayed to her throughout her childhood and beyond: always smile, always be happy and look good, no matter what is going on. Following her parents' rule to hide her real emotions and never bring up anything negative or troubling was very traumatic for Katie. Along with other repercussions of growing up in a narcissistic family, she had been experiencing CPTSD for decades. The dream she described to me had been reoccurring for more than twenty years after she left home. We discussed how Katie's parents had never valued her for who she really was as a person, but that through the recovery process she would be able to rebuild her sense of self-worth.

Gabe, forty-eight, had a reoccurring dream about struggling to clean and organize his surroundings and not fitting in with the people he encountered:

My dreams are always about trying to get things in order and feeling anxious that I can't organize everything. There are several people in the dreams, and I'm not really fitting in, but I am always trying to clean and organize things but not getting anywhere. I wake up anxious and frustrated.

Working with Gabe in therapy, we talked about what the lack of organization in his dream might represent. There were several things in his reoccurring dream that resembled his difficulties growing up in a narcissistic family. He recalled a lot of emotional chaos. He was always trying to fix things and make his parents happy, and he was the designated chore boy in charge of way too many duties for his age. Of course, he never felt he could accomplish any of these things in reality and always felt anxious and bad about himself.

Gabe also later discovered that this dream had to do with his internal disorganization and how his hypervigilant obsession with organizing everything was an effort to figure out who he was and what he wanted to do with his life. He had been so controlled by his narcissistic father, who insisted that Gabe follow a prescribed path to success, that he never had the ability to develop a strong sense of self-worth and to decide how to organize his own life.

The reoccurring dream also reflected Gabe's sense of not feeling safe. His lack of safety had many complicated parts, but the bottom line was that he was always fearful that he would somehow make a mistake and that everything in his life would fall apart.

Understanding how the various aspects of his reoccurring dream were connected to his upbringing in a narcissistic family helped to lay the foundation for Gabe's recovery process.

Jane Marie, forty-five, had an upsetting and reoccurring dream about losing her purse:

I kept dreaming almost every night about losing my purse. I was so panic-stricken in the dream because that is actually one of my biggest fears. I think of everything that's in my purse and what a nightmare it would be to replace it all. Still, the level of panic in the dream was way more frightening than my actual fear of losing everything in my wallet.

In our sessions together, Jane Marie explored her lost purse dream and realized that it signaled her fear—not of losing her purse but of being unsafe. Neglected and un-nurtured as a child of narcissistic parents, she had learned to take care of herself financially but was nonetheless left with internal security issues. Growing up, Jane Marie always felt that if something went wrong, she had no one to lean on. Her parents could not be counted on to be there for her in times of emotional need. She finally concluded that the "nightmare" she worried most about was the emptiness she felt inside, rather than a missing purse.

Physical Repercussions of CPTSD

When trauma is stored in the body, it can have physical repercussions, as evidenced in many adult children of narcissistic parents. Some report having physical symptoms that are associated with CPTSD, and some develop medical conditions.

Dr. Bessel van der Kolk is a psychiatrist and researcher who has studied post-traumatic stress disorder and wrote the best-selling book *The Body Keeps the Score*. He describes the effects of trauma on the body when it has been ongoing, such as we see with CPTSD. When the body is in a constant state of hyperalertness or hypervigilance, it has difficulty re-regulating. Dr. van der Kolk explains:

Ideally our stress hormone system should provide a lightning-fast response to threat, but then quickly return us to equilibrium. In PTSD patients, however, the stress hormone system fails at this balancing act. Fight, flight, freeze signals continue after the danger is over. . . . Instead the continued secretion of stress hormones is expressed as agitation and panic and, in the long-term, wreaks havoc with their health.[18]

Many adult children of narcissists with whom I've worked describe having various medical conditions, including autoimmune disorders; stomach issues such as irritable bowel syndrome (IBS); migraines; arthritis or other pain issues; and more. They also report that such disorders often get missed or dismissed by their medical doctors, and therefore the underlying emotional trauma is not dealt with.

Arielle Schwartz, Ph.D., explains in her online article entitled "The Neurobiology of Trauma" how the nervous system plays a role in our emotional and physiological responses to stress and trauma:

The autonomic nervous system (ANS) plays a significant role in our emotional and physiological responses to stress and trauma. The ANS is understood to have two primary systems: the sympathetic nervous system and the parasympathetic nervous system. The sympathetic nervous system is associated with the fight or flight response and the release of cortisol throughout the bloodstream. The parasympathetic nervous system puts the brakes on the sympathetic nervous system, so the body stops releasing stress chemicals and shifts toward relaxation, digestion, and regeneration. The sympathetic and parasympathetic nervous systems are meant to work in a rhythmic alternation that supports healthy digestion, sleep, and immune system functioning.[19]

We can see how stress and long-term trauma that are expressed in the form of CPTSD can interfere with a healthy emotional/physiological balance. This is why, when some people experience a CPTSD trigger, they will also report experiencing physical symptoms such as vomiting, shaking uncontrollably, back or neck pain, severe digestion issues, or fatigue they cannot explain otherwise.

Trauma and Brain Development

Research shows what is perhaps the most troubling repercussion of CPTSD: that traumatic experiences, abuse, and neglect have an adverse effect on children's brain development. As the child matures, the developing brain changes in response to the child's environment. Dr. Bruce Perry, an internationally recognized authority on brain development and children in crisis, has done pioneering research in this area. His research shows that a child's brain develops in sequence, as do other aspects of physical development. Dr. Perry points out that the sensitive brain of an infant or young child is malleable, which explains why traumatic events in a child's life, especially a young child, may change the brain's very framework.[20]

There have been volumes written about the research on trauma and brain development. While I do not proclaim to be an expert in this area, I have been struck by the research. According to an article referencing Dr. Perry's research, entitled "How Trauma Affects Child Brain Development":

When experiences are traumatic, the pathways getting the most use are those in response to the trauma; this reduces the formation of other pathways needed for adaptive behavior. Trauma in early childhood can result in disrupted attachment, cognitive delays and impaired emotional regulation.[21]

Moving On . . .

In Part Two, we have explored the impact of narcissistic parenting on children. I realize that the information and case histories are a lot to take in and process. The material I've presented may feel overwhelming, and you may have even felt hopeless at times. But there is always hope and recovery—both of which are so very important. I invite you to join me in being a hope-aholic. . . . Together we can heal and work recovery.

In Part Three: *Healing and Breaking Free*, we will begin the liberating journey of recovery from the narcissistic family dynamic you experienced in your family of origin.

Part Three

Healing and Breaking Free

Freedom is what you do with what's been done to you.

—Jean-Paul Sartre

Introduction to Part Three:

Healing and Breaking Free

Congratulations, you are now ready for recovery work. In Part One, we looked at the dynamics of a narcissistic family. In Part Two, we examined the impact of narcissistic parenting.

The good news is that it's possible to overcome the emotional and psychological damage you may have sustained as the child of a narcissistic parent by using the 5-step recovery model that I have created and used successfully for myself and hundreds of clients and workshop participants.

In Part Three, we will thoroughly explore each of the five recovery steps so that you feel confident moving forward. Each chapter will provide experiential, physical, visualization, or journaling exercises to facilitate your recovery work.

This is the practical section of the book. In offering solutions and actionable approaches to dealing with your narcissistic family experience, it is my belief that you will be well prepared to genuinely overcome the legacy of distorted, tangled love.

If you are an adult child of narcissistic parenting, you are used to the focus being on your parent while you remain either mostly invisible or beholden to your parent's needs and wishes. The best part of recovery is that you finally get to focus on *you*.

As we begin this important journey of healing, there are a few principles to keep in mind:

♦ **Focusing on you and your trauma doesn't mean you're selfish.** Some people are told that it is selfish, self-centered, or egotistical to focus on

themselves and to engage in the process of understanding their own
trauma. In fact, it is extremely important that the focus be on you when
you work the 5-step recovery model. Healing and taking good care of
yourself will improve your ability not only to lead a healthier life but to
enjoy healthier relationships.

♦ **Engaging in the recovery process does not mean you are being a victim.**
Often clients who work with me through the recovery process are initially
resistant, because they're afraid they'll get stuck in a victim mentality. So
let's be clear. In the beginning of your recovery, you are entitled to feel
like a victim, in the sense that you come to understand how you were
harmed as a child and identify what you need to work on. In order for
the recovery process to proceed, the wounded child within you needs to
be recognized and validated. But I want to assure you that when you have
completed the five steps, you will most definitely not feel like a victim.
You will feel like a more authentic, developed, whole person.

♦ **It is important to work the five steps in sequence.** There is a reason why
the five steps must be worked in sequence in order to be effective. For
each step to be beneficial, the previous step must have been completed.
You may have to go back to a step and do more work on it, but it is
important to do one step at a time, in sequence. I suggest that before you
begin the five steps, you first read all of Part Three, so that you have a
clear picture of what recovery consists of. Then you can go back and
work the steps and exercises in sequence.

♦ **Your recovery work is an inside job.** I advise you not to start family
therapy with your narcissistic parent or family until you have completed
your own recovery work. After you work the five steps, you will be in
a stronger frame of mind to try family therapy, if you choose to do so.
Usually, family therapy with a narcissist is not successful, but depending
on the severity of the parent's narcissism, some families may benefit.

♦ **Your family history may feel like a taboo subject, but it's not.** Many
adult children feel guilty discussing and processing what took place in
their family of origin. But examining our past is necessary in order for
us to understand who we are, where we came from, and what happened
to us. This is how we determine how to heal and what we need to work
on. It does not make you a bad son or daughter to review and understand
the family dynamic in which you were raised. Rather, it will help you

become your authentic self. You are dealing in a normal way with an abnormal situation.

♦ **Trust your feelings.** This will be difficult because many adult children of narcissistic parents grow up with self-doubt, unable to trust their own perceptions of reality. You may have been gaslit and told you were the crazy one, so your ability to trust what you feel may have been seriously inhibited. We will be working on strengthening your ability to trust your own feelings, but it's important to be aware of how a history of self-doubt can be a difficult challenge to overcome.

♦ **Use a journal.** I advise my clients to use a special journal for their 5-step work. This is where you will be keeping your healing work all in one place. Having the journal—or a special file on your computer—will help you to go back and see how far you have come as you proceed in the 5-step recovery process. Your journal can also be helpful if you are working with a therapist to do this work.

♦ **Work on recalling and describing your social history.** It is helpful to spend some time recalling and describing your social history from birth to the present, in order to gain a more complete understanding of your life story. Below are some general questions and issues that will help you begin this process. You can start with very brief answers and add to your history as you go. Keep it with your journal work. You don't have to complete this before working the steps; rather, you can add to it as you go.

Your Social History

Here are some general questions to begin to think about and document in your journal.

1. Where did you grow up? What kind of city, town, neighborhood?
2. Were your parents together or divorced?
3. What are your parents' names and occupations?
4. What are your siblings' names and ages?
5. What was your relationship like with your mom?
6. What was your relationship like with your dad?
7. What was your relationship like with your stepparent if you had one?

8. What were your relationships like with your siblings?

9. What was it like being an only child if you were one?

10. What comes to mind when you think of your early childhood years?

11. What comes to mind when you think of your elementary school years?

12. What comes to mind when you think of your teenage years?

13. What comes to mind when you think of your young adult years?

14. What were your first love relationships like?

15. Were there any significant traumas in your childhood other than the dysfunctional family issues?

16. What was the economic situation of your family?

17. What are the main messages you feel you got from your parents?

18. What role did you play in your family?

19. Who were the supportive people in your life as you were growing up (e.g., aunts, uncles, grandparents, teachers, friends, etc.)?

20. Describe the presence (or not) of alcohol and/or drugs in your family.

21. Describe any criminal behavior in your family.

22. Describe the presence (or not) of mental illness in the family.

23. Describe any accidents, medical issues, or early deaths in your family.

24. Did your family move a lot? If so, describe.

25. If one parent was narcissistic, was the other revolving around the narcissist and therefore enabling them?

26. Describe your parents' engulfing or ignoring behaviors.

27. Describe whether or not the children in your family were treated the same.

28. Can you identify the scapegoat, golden child, and/or lost child in your family—and if you were any of these?

29. Have you had any significant psychiatric issues, diagnoses, or mental health hospitalizations? (If so, describe.)

30. Do you overachieve or self-sabotage or both?

Keeping these questions in mind, let's move on to Part Three and your recovery work. We will start with the first step: Acceptance, Grieving, and Processing Trauma.

Chapter Nine

Step 1—Acceptance, Grieving, and Processing Trauma

Once I accepted that my father has a disorder that affects my entire family, it was easier to move on and process the trauma. I didn't want to do this at first because I found myself going back to the empty well, hoping my dad would finally change. Maybe on my birthday he'd be different. Maybe this time when I talk to him, he would get it. But now I know there is power in finally accepting the truth.

—Bernie, 38

Acceptance

The first step in recovery is accepting that your parent has a narcissistic disorder, which means that they were incapable of giving you the unconditional love, nurturing, empathy, guidance, and care that you needed as a child. Your parent was unable to meet your emotional needs, and that left you feeling abandoned and emotionally orphaned. Once you fully accept this difficult truth, you can begin the healing work.

Jerome, thirty-five, talked to me about the difficulty he had accepting the truth about his narcissistic father and enabling mother, especially when he thought about his children missing out on having loving grandparents:

*It hit me early on in recovery that I had three children who did not have
good grandparents. This kept me from acceptance for a long time. I wanted
my kids to have loving grandparents, and I felt so bad for them that this
wasn't the case. Wasn't there something I could do? But whenever my folks
were with my children, they'd be over the top with them momentarily and
then just forget about them. Mom and Dad are too into themselves to really
pay attention or care. My work in recovery was for me and for my kids. But
I have to say, acceptance took some time because I wanted to believe my
parents would be different with grandchildren than they were with me.*

Why is acceptance so hard? Because, as we learned previously, denial
is a big part of the narcissistic family system, and even adult children of
narcissistic parents don't want to give up the hope that things will get
better. As Bernie and Jerome describe, we tend to want to keep wishing
and hoping that our relationship with our narcissistic parent or parents
will change. We all want to be part of a warm, loving family, and if we've
never experienced being in such a family, it is hard to accept that reality.
We may also get caught up in the codependent mindset that maybe we
can fix our parent's behavior by being a better son or daughter or achieving more so our parent will finally be proud of us—and love us the way
we yearn to be loved.

It may be easy to say, "They did the best they could," and just let it
go. Maybe our parents did do the best they could with what they had,
but that doesn't erase the trauma they imposed on their children. And,
a lot of times, they *didn't* do the best they could with what they had; in
fact, they were downright abusive in many ways. As adult children, we
often hear people advise us to "just get over it already . . . the past is the
past." But we know it doesn't work that way. The trauma is still there; we
experienced emotional abuse when we were children, and we can never
condone child abuse.

Truly accepting that our parent has a narcissistic disorder means that
we have to give up the expectation of getting what we always wanted from
them—and still want. Then we have to deal with the trauma that is still
present within ourselves. In learning to accept that our narcissistic parent
is incapable of giving us the love we always wanted, it may be helpful to
think of this metaphorical example: A person has been given the gift of a

beautiful bicycle, but they are literally unable to get on the bike and ride it. Something is holding them back, and they simply don't have the capacity to ride their beautiful bike. Similarly, a narcissistic parent has a beautiful child but is unable to love that child properly. Their narcissistic disorder is holding them back. Although children of narcissistic parents understandably expect their parent to pay attention to them, to love and nurture them, the parent's narcissistic disorder renders them incapable of doing so.

Accepting the truth of how we were treated by our narcissistic parents doesn't mean that we should blame or hate them. Acceptance means understanding our parents' limitations so that we can begin our healing. Most children, including those in narcissistic families, do love their parents. But in the narcissistic family it is the parents who are not properly loving their children, and the children cannot help but react to that improper loving. Again, children of narcissistic parents are reacting in a normal way to an abnormal situation. With that said, as adults we are responsible for our own healing and recovery; blame and hate don't help in that process.

It is important to remember that narcissism is a spectrum disorder, so there can be varying degrees of narcissistic traits. People on the lower end of the spectrum may be able to authentically confront their behavior and engage in therapy; for those kinds of parents, there may be some hope for change. It is helpful to determine if your parent has only a few narcissistic traits, is further along the spectrum, or has full-blown narcissistic personality disorder. You may want to refer to the "Narcissistic Personality Disorder Diagnostic Criteria" (from the *Diagnostic and Statistical Manual of Mental Disorders*) in the Appendix to help you determine this.

How Do You Work on Acceptance?

In order to begin the process of acceptance, it is important to determine the greatest barriers to accepting that your parent has a narcissistic disorder. There will be reasons why you are struggling with accepting this truth about your family, and it is important to figure out what those reasons are. What are the barriers keeping you from acknowledging and accepting the truth of your family history?

To help you assess your barriers to acceptance, I have provided a journal exercise below, which includes various relevant topics and questions. Write as much as you can about these issues and how they impact your concerns about accepting your parent's narcissism. If you are in therapy, discuss these issues with your therapist.

Many adult children from narcissistic families are afraid that they might be wrong in their assessment of their parent or family. Remember: your feelings, perceptions, and memories are yours. Feelings cannot be wrong. Remember, too, that you can love your parent and still accept that they have narcissistic traits or a full-blown narcissistic personality disorder. Acknowledging this reality does not make you a bad person.

Journal Topics and Questions on Acceptance

Writing on the following topics and questions in your journal will help you with the process of acceptance. You may want to begin with those questions or topics that you feel are the easiest to deal with. You can later come back to the issues that may be more challenging.

+ Do I want to be accountable for my own feelings and work on them?
+ Am I letting myself trust my own feelings?
+ What does it say about me if I accept that my parent has a narcissistic disorder, couldn't love me the way I needed to be loved as a child, and will likely never change?
+ If I accept that my parent has a narcissistic disorder, does that mean I am unlovable?
+ If I accept that my parent has a narcissistic disorder, does that mean there is something wrong with me?
+ If I accept that my parent has a narcissistic disorder, does that mean I'm crazy?
+ Do I keep wishing and hoping my narcissistic parent will change?
+ If I accept that my parent has a narcissistic disorder, am I afraid it will lead to more abandonment from my parents and/or siblings?
+ Do I continue to have expectations of my parents? What are those expectations?

- Am I afraid of what others will think of me if I accept that my parent has a narcissistic disorder?
- If I accept that my parent has a narcissistic disorder, what if I am wrong?
- Am I fearful that I am a narcissist? (Hint: If you can provide empathy to others and tune in to the emotional world of others, you are not a narcissist.)

How Do I Know When I Have Accepted That My Parent Has a Narcissistic Disorder?

You will know you have mastered acceptance when you no longer expect your parent to be able to tune in to you and provide empathy and support for the real you. You will simply accept them for who they are, even if you don't like their behavior or the way they treat you. One thing to watch out for is transferring the deep need to feel loved by your parent(s) to someone else, like a friend or partner. Of course, we all want to feel loved by friends and partners, but no one can really replace the love we needed from our parents. We will be learning how to re-parent ourselves as we progress through the five steps.

Denise, forty, is the adult child of two narcissistic parents. When she had finally mastered acceptance, she was able to share this breakthrough with me:

Now when I call my parents to check in with them, I know they will not ask about me or the kids or how we are doing. I expect that they will just talk about themselves and assume I will listen to them. I no longer hang up frustrated and sad, I just know and accept that it will be this way.

Daniel, thirty-two, who has struggled with accepting the truth about his narcissistic father, told me how his expectations have changed dramatically:

In the past, I would feel an emptiness when my dad ignored my birthday and other important events in my life. I'd receive a card or call from my mom, but never anything from him. Now I don't expect it anymore. He just is who he is. It's sad, but it's a relief to let go of my unrealistic expectations.

Grieving

Once you have accepted the reality of growing up with a narcissistic parent in a narcissistic family, you will be ready to initiate the second part of Step One, which is grieving and processing trauma.

When I speak of grieving, I am referring to mourning the loss of the parent and family that you wanted and deserved but never had. The natural grieving process, as written about by Dr. Elisabeth Kübler-Ross in her book *On Death and Dying*,[22] consists of five stages: denial, anger, bargaining, depression, and acceptance. In grieving for the parent you wanted and never had, we will use these stages, too, but acceptance is the first step since we already engaged in denial and bargaining when we were growing up with a narcissistic parent. Without acceptance we cannot move on to deal with our true feelings of grief. Let's look at some examples of how the stages of grief work for the adult child of narcissistic parents.

Stages of Grief

1. Acceptance: We begin by accepting that our parent's narcissistic disorder resulted in their limited capacity to be a loving, nurturing parent.
2. Denial: As young children, in order to survive we had to deny the reality of our parent's inability to properly love us. We assumed this was how parents acted.
3. Bargaining: As children and adolescents, we kept wishing and hoping our narcissistic parent would change, and we tried numerous strategies in order to win their love and approval.
4. Anger: As adult children, when we realize the extent of our narcissistic parent's lack of love, support, and caring, we may feel intense anger at how their neglect affected our lives in severe, adverse ways.
5. Depression: There is usually an intense sadness that comes with grieving the vision of the parent we never had and the family we always wished we had.

An effective way to initiate the grieving process is to consider the questions and topics in the following journal exercise.

Journal Questions and Topics on Grieving

Writing on the following topics and questions in your journal will help you with the process of grieving. Take your time with this journaling and allow yourself to be true to your feelings. Know you are not alone in this process and remind yourself it is okay for you to have the courage to stand in your own truth.

- The ideal parent I wished I had would be . . .
- What was my narcissistic parent really like?
- The ideal family I wished I had would be . . .
- What was my family really like?
- How were my parents different in public from how they were behind closed doors?
- Write about the little boy or girl you didn't get to be.
- Write about what you missed as a child that you needed or wanted.
- Complete this sentence: When I grieve the loss of the parent or family I didn't have, I feel . . .

You can add to this list with whatever comes up for you as you progress through the five steps.

Processing Trauma

Grieving the loss of the family you always wanted but never had brings up the trauma you experienced as the child of a narcissistic parent. Learning to confront and process that trauma, which you have stored up since childhood, is a crucial part of Step One.

To effectively process what you experienced in your family of origin, you need to authentically feel the feelings related to the trauma. And since you will be processing an entire lifetime of experiences, emotions, memories, and events, this won't happen overnight. You'll be tuning in to your wounded child, allowing that child to feel anger, rage, sadness, loss, abandonment, and aloneness. You may have repressed a lot of emotions over the years or have been told that your feelings are not important, so it may be difficult to allow these deep, troubling feelings to surface. Some people have to teach themselves to feel again, as they initially feel numb when thinking about how they felt growing up. Working with a therapist while processing the trauma can be very helpful, and I strongly encourage you to do so, as it is important to have another person validating your wounded child. Being receptive to the child within you means that you are allowing that child to have a voice and to say, "It was not okay how I was treated."

When she began her recovery, Marcy, forty-four, talked about "forgetting how to cry" and the fear she felt as a consequence of having held in her feelings for most of her life:

I'm so afraid that if I let myself cry and really feel this stuff, I will never stop. I'm afraid I will get stuck there. I was taught for so long to suck it up and that my feelings didn't matter. I forgot how to cry. I let myself start crying and then stop myself. It's like there's a danger sign that goes off in my brain that says "Don't do that or you will get in trouble and be shamed again."

A number of my clients began their recovery work when they became parents for the first time. They report to me that when experiencing the initial wave of unconditional love for their child, it dawned on them that their parents probably never felt that kind of love for them. They feel a profound sadness and wonder, "Why didn't my parents have this kind of deep love for me?"

Sherri, twenty-nine, recalled how she got in touch with the trauma of having grown up without the unconditional love she now feels for her own daughter:

When my baby girl was born, I was terrified at first that I would be like my narcissistic mother and harm her in some way. This caused me to get really serious about my recovery work. I was thrilled when I felt that rush of unconditional love for my baby, and at the same time heartbroken because I felt so sorry for the hurt child inside me. The kid who yearned for her mother to hug her and tell her everything would be okay, instead of ignoring her or yelling at her and calling her a crybaby. This is when I realized my own trauma.

You will likely have PTSD reactions as you bring up traumatic memories, and it is important to let that happen. It is helpful to schedule quiet time alone on a regular basis for this deep recovery work.

When working on processing the trauma, if you are in a love relationship, it is important to advise your partner what you are doing and why. A partner can be very supportive of this process if they understand it. If they don't, you could get messages to "get over it already," which are not helpful. If you don't process the trauma, you won't be able to move on to the next step successfully. Sometimes when working with a client who was raised in a narcissistic family, I will bring in the partner to explain some of the 5-step work so that they can be supportive and not give the wrong messages or worry too much about their partner's going through this process.

Processing deep feelings associated with the trauma of growing up with a narcissistic parent can be very difficult, and many people at first don't want to engage in this part of their recovery. Or they think that because they have already told some of their childhood stories to a friend or loved one or therapist, they don't have to go any further or deeper. Which is why I often find myself repeatedly redirecting clients back to this step. You may find yourself moving on to the next step and then realizing that you have to come back to Step One to further process traumatic feelings. I have had a number of clients work on this step for a year or more.

Some people report that they can recall very few memories of their childhood. If that is the case for you, you can still write about how you felt as a child, even if you don't have a specific story to go with every feeling. If you are finding it difficult to access your feelings, it can be helpful to watch movies about dysfunctional families and allow yourself to cry. This may jump-start the process for you.

Journal work is extremely helpful in processing trauma. Think of as many stories about your childhood as you can, and as you write about them in the journal exercise below, try to remember how it felt to experience them. Really *feel* those feelings. You can also write in your journal as if you are talking to your wounded inner child, giving them the empathy they deserve.

Journal Topics and Questions for Processing Trauma

♦ Write about the negative messages you may have internalized as a child. Where did they come from and why? How do you feel about those messages now?
♦ Write about how your parent treated you and why that made you sad.
♦ Write about how your parent treated you and why that made you angry.
♦ Write about how you felt when you had to keep your feelings to yourself.
♦ Write about what you did as a child to soothe yourself when you didn't feel loved.
♦ Write about what happened to you when you expressed your feelings.
♦ Write about specific experiences from your childhood that made you feel fearful, lost, or alone.
♦ Write, in the voice of your wounded child, your feelings of anger, rage, fear, sadness, loss, abandonment, and aloneness.
♦ Write to your wounded child, empathizing with them regarding painful childhood experiences they went through.

Physical and Experiential Exercise

Sometimes doing something physical while processing trauma can be helpful and therapeutic. Since trauma gets stored in our bodies, thinking about feelings while physically working out can be a way to coax the feelings out of the body. And there are other experiences you can undertake that may also help you access and/or process your emotions.

The following are suggestions for engaging in physical or experiential exercise:

♦ Take long walks or runs while thinking about your loss.
♦ Talk to an empty chair as if it were your parent or family member and

say out loud what you want to express to that person about how you were treated growing up.

♦ Engage in any activity that causes you to be physical, such as yoga, Pilates, swimming, dancing, tennis, basketball, gardening . . . and notice what feelings come up for you afterward.

♦ Hit a boxing bag or kick lightweight boxes and notice what feelings arise.

♦ Punch pillows and notice what feelings come up.

♦ Listen to melancholy music and feel free to cry out loud.

♦ Write letters to parents and siblings expressing your sadness and anger. Do this as a cathartic way to get out your feelings, but don't send the letters. They're for therapeutic purposes only.

♦ Consider EMDR (eye movement desensitization and reprocessing) in order to access deep feelings. This is an effective trauma treatment using rapid eye movements but must be done with a trained clinician. You can go to EMDRIA.org to find a therapist in your area. You will want to make sure the EMDR therapist is also trained in treating adult children of narcissistic parents.

How Do I Know When I Have Completed My Grieving and Trauma Processing Work?

This is a difficult question to assess. If you're not sure that you've completed this part of Step One, you probably haven't. Most clients don't spend enough time on this step and have to keep going back to it for a while. If this is true for you, don't get discouraged. It is normal. When you are ready to move on, you will find that you are less emotional and not triggered as easily by people or circumstances that remind you of past trauma in your narcissistic family.

Some clients report that they didn't see the benefits of giving this process more time until after they had put in that time. Then they reported the success. For instance, Brianna, forty-five, told me how she went from hating this difficult step to feeling "lighter" and better than ever:

I hated this part of the recovery. It was so hard to feel all those feelings and work through them, but every day got better and better and I started feeling lighter . . . like I was dropping pounds of trauma from my body. It felt so good to release it all and accept my own feelings and validate my pain.

Lonnie, fifty, reported getting through the wrenching process of feeling his "gut feelings":

It felt like I was carrying the shame of my whole family in my gut. Just letting myself feel was such a relief, even though I had to force myself to do it, because it definitely wasn't easy. There was so much dysfunction in my family, and I seemed to absorb it and blame myself. I realized that I always had a stomachache after something bad happened in my family—and then with other people in my life. As I started to acknowledge and understand and accept my feelings, the stomachaches decreased. I thought the whole journal-writing thing was kind of silly at first, but when I taught myself to write in the journal and then sit with those feelings, I got it. It made sense because it worked. I really am feeling better after doing the work.

Eileen, forty-four, revealed how threatened she felt initially when I encouraged her to really feel her feelings. She courageously stuck to her recovery process, however, and is reaping the benefits:

Doing this deep feeling work was super-hard for me. We couldn't show feelings in our family growing up. If I even frowned, I would be slapped in the face and told to "put a smile on that little face of yours!" So, in recovery, even though I understood the information about the narcissistic family dynamic, allowing my feelings to come out was very hard for me. I had to learn to get out of my head and into my gut and heart.

Tara, forty-one, grew up in a family where she was only allowed to express emotion that mirrored what her narcissistic mother was feeling. Having begun to process her traumatic past, Tara is now able to embrace her own authentic feelings:

If my mom was feeling sad, I had to be sad. If she was in one of her rare good moods, I could be relatively happy. But it was never what I was really feeling, because I couldn't tell what my actual feelings were. When I first

started facing my past, I would have triggers that lasted for days. But now
I'm finally able to own my feelings. I can talk about them and accept them,
and I feel proud of myself for doing this work.

Temporary Separation from Your Narcissistic Parent

Making the decision whether or not to have contact with your narcissistic parent is not part of your recovery work until Step Four, but I often advise clients to maintain a temporary separation when beginning this first step. The reason is so that the adult child can process the trauma without getting triggered by the person who has hurt them. Sometimes this is not possible; but if it is, it seems to benefit the recovery process to temporarily separate from the narcissistic parent.

You can let your narcissistic parent know that you are working on yourself, that you need some space, and will be in touch when you can. This can be done in person or in an email, but with little drama or emotion. It is not advisable to tell your parent what you are working on. Just let them know that you love them but that you need a break for a while to take care of yourself. You don't have to explain why. If you cannot do this, try to have minimal contact. The point is to put yourself in an emotional space where you are not getting triggered and can focus on yourself.

Moving On ...

Now that you have allowed yourself to accept, grieve, and process the trauma you experienced as a child, you are ready to move to *Step Two—Separation and Individuation*. You have accomplished the most important step of your recovery, and the next steps will be easier for you to master. Give yourself a lot of credit for working hard on Step One. You have made a conscious commitment to process your trauma, and it is the key to your recovery.

Let's now move on to the important work of psychologically separating from your parents and attaining a clearer sense of self. You are well on your way to a healthier and happier you.

Chapter Ten

Step 2—Separation and Individuation

Now I am able to step back and watch the antics play out in my family in a more objective way. I feel more detached and no longer triggered by their bat-shit crazy behavior. I don't get pulled in anymore. What a relief!

—Anastasia, 66

The goal of Step Two is to work toward fully separating psychologically from your narcissistic family and its dynamics in order to become your own person. This step is marked by focused detachment from your family's behavioral patterns, to the extent that you can observe the dysfunction without getting hooked into it. When you can realistically separate the "me" from "them," your recovery begins to take hold.

Acknowledging that you come from your particular family but no longer want to have your adult identity shaped by that family means that you can be both "a part of and apart from" them. Separation and individuation do not mean geographical distance. This step involves internal, psychological work in order to see yourself as a separate person from your family of origin, free yourself from the family dynamic, and begin to define your individuated self.

Remember the prior example of imagining your family on a stage acting out their dynamics, while you are simply in the audience watching the play—no longer one of the characters playing an assigned role? When you can objectively observe your family and extricate yourself from the drama, you'll feel the sense of freedom and relief that Anastasia referred to.

Letting Go of the Role You Played

As discussed in Part Two, we tend to be saddled with a particular role when we are raised in a narcissistic family. These dysfunctional roles rarely honor or reflect who a child really is. By now, you have likely identified the role you played in your family, whether it was the scapegoat, lost child, golden child, only child, or different roles at different times. Now is the time in your recovery process to cast aside the role that was assigned to you and just be you. Having played along with the role(s) by which your family defined you for most of your life, you can now work on letting go of that inauthentic identity and finally defining the person you truly are.

You can begin with the following journal exercise concerning the role(s) you played in your narcissistic family and the identity you now envision for yourself.

Journal Topics and Questions on Your Role in the Family

- What was my most prominent role in my family of origin?
- How do I feel about that role?
- How do I think it harmed me to have to play a role?
- Who in the family keeps me in that role now?
- How/why does that person continue to force me into that role?
- How does each member of my family define me? How would they describe me?
- How do I want to describe myself now?
- What is the story that my family tells about me? Do I agree with it?
- What is my story about growing up in my family?

Anthony, forty-four, came to understand that he was the scapegoat in his family. He had a narcissistic father and an enabling mother, and both seemed to blame family problems on him. He realized in his recovery work that although he could not change them, he could change himself and his own reactions to them:

*I never could understand why my sister was the favored child and I always
got in trouble for everything. Even to this day, if something goes wrong, they
look to me first and ask what I did or said. They assume I screwed things up.
It always felt like my family just didn't like me. For so many years, I internalized their judgment of me and believed that something really was wrong
with me. Now I understand that I was the kid that got handed the scapegoat
role—particularly when Dad was in a bad mood or feeling mad about something. Mom didn't necessarily blame me, but she didn't protect me either.
Now that I have worked my recovery, I don't allow myself to believe that
I'm the bad guy, and I don't let myself get triggered by my family anymore.
I've learned how to trust my own feelings and my own sense of reality. If
anyone in the family tries to lay that "screwup" role on me, I can actually
kind of laugh it off and tell myself, "There they go again!"*

Fortunately, in Anthony's recovery he learned that his parents no
longer defined him. He became empowered to determine his own worth.

Owning Your Uniqueness

How are you unique and different from your narcissistic parent and the
other members of your family? In the process of individuating, it's important to consider the traits, values, and behaviors that are authentically
yours or that you want to further develop. And it's also helpful to think
critically about the values, traits, and behaviors of your family members
and to decide which of those represent who you are or want to be as an
individual, versus those you want to reject.

In discovering and learning to own her uniqueness, Whitney, twenty-
nine, told me about how she had struggled to define herself despite her
narcissistic father's disapproval and her mother's habitual reinforcement
of her father's directives and opinions:

*My dad wanted me to follow in the family business. I'm the only child, so
I was his only hope of continuing the name he had made for himself in
our community. I never showed any interest in the business, but he kept
assuming I'd fall into line. It wasn't only that I had no interest in the type of*

business Dad ran; I didn't agree with his values and how they played out in
what he had accomplished. After I graduated and told my parents I was set
on pursuing my own career, they both basically turned on me. I had dis-
graced them by refusing what they had always planned for me. I'm now the
black sheep but I'm learning to respect my decision.

Many adult children of narcissists call themselves the "black sheep" of
the family, realizing that somehow they didn't fit in. When they break the
rules by not conforming to the expected mold of the family dynamics, or
by truthfully calling out the family's dysfunction, the other members will
often turn on them. To illustrate the courage it takes to individuate and call
out the truth, I encourage adult children from narcissistic families to think
of themselves metaphorically not as black sheep but as giraffes. The giraffe
is farsighted, sees things sheep can't see, is both grounded and powerful. A
giraffe's expansive perspective allows for a more accurate picture of its environment. In the next chapter, you'll learn more about what this unique
animal can represent for adult children of narcissists, but at this point you
can begin to define your own uniqueness in the journal exercise below.

Journal Topics and Questions on Owning Your Uniqueness

♦ How would I describe my narcissistic parent in terms of their traits,
   values, and behaviors?
♦ How would I describe my enabling parent in terms of their traits, values,
   and behaviors?
♦ How would I describe my siblings in terms of their traits, values, and
   behaviors?
♦ How would I describe how I am different from each of the members of
   my family when it comes to my traits, values, and behaviors?
♦ What values are important to me but not to other members of my family?
♦ What activities are important to me but not to other members of my
   family?
♦ What are some things I learned in my family that I am choosing to
   keep in my belief system? (For example: religion, politics, economics,
   education.)

Opting Out of Triangulation

At this point in your recovery, it is important to closely monitor communication with your family. Take particular note of how much triangulation is going on. Remember the game of telephone and the indirect communication we discussed earlier? Are the people in your family still not talking directly with each other but rather going through other family members to get their message across? It is time to take yourself out of your family's triangulated communication.

How do you do this? Simply state that you will not take part in talking about or hearing about other members behind their back. When someone in the family talks to you about someone else, you politely say that you believe this is between them and the person they are referring to and that you would prefer they talk to that person directly. You are no longer the middle guy who is expected to carry the message to the person being talked about.

Peter, thirty-five, was the one other family members went to when they were upset with someone else in the family. He got all the frustration, anger, sadness, and bad feelings dumped on him. He would repeatedly get hooked into the triangulation process and proceed to call members of the family to try to set them straight, a frustrating and fruitless effort to say the least. Then he learned how unhealthy engaging in triangulation was for him:

What am I? The family therapist? I got really tired of being the constant mediator and teacher in the family. I used to take this on and try to help and fix and make things right. It never turned out well and often got turned back on me. I was thrilled to learn in therapy that this was not my job. I could stop doing it and that was actually healthy for me. Now when it happens, and yes it still does, I just calmly say that they need to speak to each other directly and I don't want to be involved. I liberated myself from the whole deal, and it feels so good. I'm so much less emotionally exhausted now, and now I can finally focus on my own life.

Journal Topics and Questions on
Opting Out of Triangulation

+ How would I describe how triangulation works in my family?
+ Who in the family seems to engage in triangulation the most?
+ Am I struggling to opt out of the triangulation in my family? If so, why?
+ Do I find myself addicted to the gossip and drama in my family? If so, why?
+ Am I having trouble setting boundaries to prevent triangulation? If so, why?

Becoming Aware of the Narcissist's Projected Feelings

We've learned that narcissists project their feelings onto others because they are not good at embracing and facing their own emotions. So, for example, when the narcissist gets upset about something in their own life, they take those feelings out on other people. During this step of recovery, it is time to be very aware of such projected feelings.

Let's say the narcissistic father had a bad day at work and comes home angry. He takes his anger out on other family members by yelling at them, criticizing them, or putting them down in some way. Or the narcissistic mother is tired and depressed, but instead of working on her own feelings, she starts picking on other family members, giving them the message that they are not good enough. What she is really feeling is that she herself is not good enough, but she has to project that onto others. Remember, at the core of the narcissist is a very fragile ego that is often covered up by their grandiosity. Their own self-loathing gets projected onto others in the family.

Part of the work in this step is to notice when your narcissistic parent engages in projecting their feelings onto others. When you are the target of this projection, it often feels like it comes out of the blue, and it's confusing because the accusation or criticism has nothing to do with you. When the narcissist's projected feelings come at you, take a step back and ask yourself: *Does this have anything to do with me or something I did?*

A narcissistic parent can also engage in positive projection. This occurs when the parent idealizes someone in the family, such as the golden child.

Positive projection is usually based on the narcissist's bad feelings about themselves or on good qualities they have but are uncomfortable embracing. Adult children of narcissists often report that they were the victims of both positive and negative projection, as the narcissistic parent may have idealized them one day and devalued them the next. Remember, projection is about the narcissist's casting their particular emotions onto someone else and being unable to acknowledge that they are doing so.

The skill you need to learn here is to identify when your narcissistic parent is projecting their feelings onto you and to tell yourself: *This has nothing to do with me. It is something that is going on inside my parent, and I do not have to let it affect me.*

Priscilla, forty-four, reported how she has learned to deal with her narcissistic mother's tendency to project negative feelings onto others:

When our narcissist mother had a bad day, we would all pay. She'd walk in the door, clearly upset about something that happened at work, and launch into an angry tirade, criticizing me and my sister for whatever struck her at the time—our failure to put the clean dishes away, books left on the table where we were studying. She'd go on and on, and I'd feel upset for the rest of the evening. She never apologized. Now if we're together and I hear her going off like that, I just smile, because I know her anger has nothing to do with me and, sadly, everything to do with her own unhappiness.

Gary, forty-three, has a similar story about having learned through Step Two to recognize that his narcissistic father's projected feelings had little to do with him:

My dad would be in the dumps and feeling sorry for himself about something and then out of nowhere he would accuse me of acting sad and tell me to buck up and be grateful. I'd be like . . . what? I don't feel sad, what is he talking about? Now I understand what was going on. He was handing off his dark moods to me. I don't fall for that anymore.

Krista, thirty-six, was an only child of a narcissistic mother and held several roles in her family. She reports how confusing her mom's positive and negative projection was for her:

On the good days, when Mom was in her superficial grandiosity state, I was the best kid, best student, smartest of all my cousins; but on her bad days I was harshly criticized for everything I did or said. According to her, I was either absolutely exceptional or absolutely terrible. It really confused me until I figured out that my mom's projected image of me, which depended on her emotional state at the time, had nothing to do with me.

The goal of Step Two is to see your narcissistic parent's projected feelings for what they are and to no longer allow their misplaced emotional outbursts to hurt you. You are able to tune in to the fact that when they project their unhappiness onto you, it's their problem, not yours.

Journal Topics and Questions on Becoming Aware of the Narcissist's Projected Feelings

+ Was I blamed for things that had nothing to do with me? (Give examples.)
+ What effect did my narcissistic parent's projection have on me?
+ How do I feel about my parent projecting their emotions onto me as a child and now as an adult?
+ Write about how you are understanding projection better now and seeing it for what it is.
+ Write about feeling less confused now about how your narcissistic parent projected their emotions onto you.
+ Write about feeling less self-doubt now that you understand how your parent projected emotions onto you.
+ Write about feeling less controlled by your narcissistic parent now that you understand the projection process.

Overcoming a Narcissistic Parent's Envy

We've discussed how strange it is for a parent to be jealous of their own child. Remember, the message one gets in a narcissistic family is that you are supposed to be good at certain things in order to make the narcissistic parent feel good about themselves, but you are not supposed to outshine them. It's a crazy mixed message. *Be good, but don't be better than your narcissistic parent* because then you'll become the target of their irrational jealousy.

I have found that often clients don't recognize a narcissistic parent's envy because if you grow up with the message that you are not good enough, it is hard to believe that anyone could be jealous of you. But a narcissistic parent's envy is actually another form of projection, based on that parent's lack of self-esteem. When you can separate yourself from your family's dynamics, you can more easily recognize a parent's envy and the damage it has done. Prior to completing Step Two's separation and individuation, it is common for adult children to blame themselves or allow themselves to be blamed for their parent's jealousy.

Martin's story is a case in point. Both of his narcissistic parents became envious of their son's academic accomplishments. Although they expected him to go to college and have a successful career, his postgraduate choices led to family disharmony:

> *All was good when I got my bachelor's degree and even when I got my master's, but when I started working on my doctorate, my parents both discouraged me, told me to drop out, and let me know that they would not support my continuing education. They had graduate degrees but not a doctorate. Now I had gone too far. In not-so-subtle ways, they communicated to me that I was getting a "big head" by striving to further my academic status. They didn't come right out and say it, but their underlying feeling was: "Who do you think you are?" Prior to my recovery, I probably would have bought into their way of thinking and dropped out of grad school. I would have blamed myself for making them feel bad by going further than they had. Thank goodness for my recovery work because I could now see their envy for what it is and just do what I needed to do for myself without feeling guilty or worrying that I am hurting their feelings.*

Lauren, thirty-three, was constantly nagged by her narcissistic mother about her weight. She was put on diets at very young ages, and all her mother talked or cared about was Lauren's appearance. In her early twenties, Lauren joined a gym and got into great shape with a special trainer she loved. At the same time, her mother had put on some weight. Now instead of being happy for her daughter, Lauren's mother couldn't handle the fact that Lauren looked better than she did:

After my weight loss and fitness work, whenever I'd see Mom, she would call me anorexic. I've never had an eating disorder of any kind, but she would say things like "Get your anorexic, skinny butt over here and do the dishes for me." It was so hurtful. Why couldn't she just be proud of me? I had always doubted myself, and I wondered if maybe Mom was right about this, too—was I losing too much weight? But thankfully, I am doing my recovery work now and can see that my mom is just jealous, so it doesn't hurt me anymore. I think it is sad for her, but I get to be me and that includes being the best me I can be.

Joaquin, fifty-five, came from a family that didn't have much money when he was growing up. They lived in small rented houses or apartments and had little in the way of material things. As an adult, Joaquin became a successful dentist and was able to buy a lovely, and expensive, home for his family, which provoked envy in his narcissistic father. His dad had always been envious of Joaquin's accomplishments, and he continued to project his own lack of self-esteem by belittling his son's achievements:

My dad's ego could not handle our beautiful home. Whenever they came to visit us, instead of being proud and happy for us, he would make comments about what he didn't like about the house. He'd say things like "This kitchen is so big it seems like it's just for show." Or he'd comment about our décor saying our contemporary furniture was "cheap-looking." It used to really bother us, but now my wife and I know it is just his jealousy, so we ignore it. It took me a long time to get to this place of separation from my narcissistic father, and to understand that this was about his fragile ego and had nothing to do with us.

Journal Topics and Questions on Overcoming a Narcissistic Parent's Envy

♦ Write about times when you felt your narcissistic parent was envious of you.
♦ How did my parent's envy make me feel?

+ Did I feel guilty when I achieved something that my parent never achieved? (If so, describe how you felt.)
+ How did my parent's envy hurt me?
+ Are my siblings jealous of me? How might their jealousy be related to the narcissistic parent's envy?

Talking Back to Internalized Negative Messages

In Step One we worked on identifying your most prominent internalized negative messages. Now it is time to start talking back to those messages and changing them into positive statements. While this can be a difficult process, with practice it can be done. You will need to use your adult paternal or maternal voice to talk to your inner wounded child. Think of this as if you are speaking to a child who is hurt, telling them they are lovable, worthy, and good enough. Merely using affirmations won't work because you won't really believe them yet. So you have to use logic that comes from your adult self, explaining to your wounded child why those prior negative messages that you inherited in your narcissistic family are wrong.

Journal Topics on Talking Back to Internalized Negative Messages

+ Write a "script" in which your *internalized negative message* is one character, and *you* are the other character. The dialogue will consist of the internalized message guy spewing negativity, and you talking back with your reasoned, self-compassionate statements.
+ Rewrite your most prominent internalized negative messages, changing them into the messages you want to send yourself.
+ Write a letter to your wounded child about each negative message you received from your narcissistic parent—and explain why that message is wrong. As you are writing the letter to your wounded child, picture yourself actually talking to a child and reassuring them.

Remember, you received the negative messages about yourself from emotionally unhealthy parents. They were in no position to judge you or define who you are. Remind yourself that none of us should take counsel from the wounded.

If you are having trouble with this journal exercise, consider seeking an EMDR therapist to help you. EMDR (eye movement desensitization and reprocessing) can help desensitize the negative messages and reinforce the positive messages you want to send yourself.

Challenging the Family Mantra

A narcissistic family often has a mantra or an informal code of beliefs, which the children are taught to believe in. It is time to challenge that mantra if you no longer believe it or now realize it was wrong.

Given that children in a narcissistic family are taught the wrong definition of love, perhaps your family's mantra was something like *You are valued for what you* do—*rather than for who you are.* Many adult children of narcissistic parents are told that their family is better than others. Some learn that what is most important is how you look, not how you feel. Many are taught to be stoic and not show feelings because to do so means you're weak, as well as a burden to the parents. And if children of narcissists express troubled feelings, they may be told they are being too sensitive.

In thinking about your narcissistic parent and your family of origin, was there a mantra or were there a number of mantras instilled in you? Was there a particular narrative about your family that you were taught to believe? Do you still believe this? Now is the time to confront these beliefs.

When she was growing up, Allison, twenty-five, was taught by her narcissistic mother that her family was better than other families and that there were certain children she couldn't play with because, in her mother's words, they were "not our kind of people." During her Step Two work, Allison learned to change the mantra she grew up with to one that more accurately reflected her own beliefs:

Sometimes I had friends who didn't have as much money as we had. My mother discouraged me from hanging out with them, and when I asked her why, she'd say, "They're just not our kind of people." As I got older, I understood more clearly what that meant: that I could only be friends with kids who lived in an upper-middle-class neighborhood like ours. I don't believe this anymore. When it comes to choosing friends, if I had to define my mantra now it would be: I judge people on the quality of their character.

Brad, forty-six, grew up in a very athletic family with a narcissistic father who placed a high value on being trim and physically fit. Anyone overweight or whose appearance was less than ideal was looked down on. Brad realized in his recovery that he no longer believed that *staying fit and trim is of the utmost importance*, which had been his dad's mantra for as long as Brad could remember:

My dad was really critical of overweight people, and we grew up almost discriminating against them. His strong message was: it's all about how you look. Not only did this cause me to be a perfectionist, but it caused me to be more focused on my looks than who I am as a man and a person. I don't want my kids to have that kind of pressure, and I want them to learn to value people for who they are as human beings.

Scott, fifty-one, came from a family whose mantra was: *Keep your feelings to yourself.* His narcissistic father would typically call him a baby or a weak person if Scott expressed how he felt. In recovery, Scott learned that his feelings were a burden to his father because his dad didn't know how to handle them. As he discovered the importance of identifying his feelings and sharing them with people he trusted—even though it was initially difficult to do so—Scott felt a great sense of relief:

I thought it was just a man thing. Big boys don't cry; boys are supposed to be tough. But, as I grew up, got married, and had kids of my own, I could see that this is a wrong message. I needed to express my feelings to my wife, and I wanted to teach my kids the importance of this also. I now realize that being able to discuss feelings is really a super-strength and makes me a better person, father, and husband.

Journal Topics and Questions on Challenging
the Family Mantra

- What was our family mantra?
- Which family member pushed this mantra the most?
- Why do I still believe this mantra?
- Why don't I believe this mantra anymore?
- What do I want the mantra to be for me and my own family now?

Breaking Free from Being Engulfed or Ignored

As we discussed in Part Two, a narcissistic parent can be engulfing or ignoring or sometimes both. As an adult child having grown up with these dysfunctional parenting dynamics, your work toward separation and individuation can be challenging because both engulfing and ignoring parents thwart your ability to develop a sense of self. If you were ignored, you were spending your time and energy just trying to gain your parent's love and attention. If you were engulfed, you were told what to do, think, be, wear, and believe in. Both kinds of parenting interfered with your emotional development, which is why I say the impact of the opposite is the same.

By now, you have likely determined if you were engulfed, ignored, or both by your narcissistic parent. In this part of your recovery, you will be undoing this dynamic so you can work on yourself. If you were ignored as a child, the recovery work is to accept that past reality and to stop trying to get the attention and approval from your dysfunctional family. Instead, you can start giving that loving attention and approval to yourself. If you were engulfed as a child, the work is to separate yourself psychologically from all the demands that your narcissistic parent placed on you regarding how to be and what to believe. Instead, you can begin the process of determining how *you* want to be and what *you* want to believe in.

Janice, thirty-seven, is working on psychologically separating from her engulfing narcissistic mother and becoming her own person. After a lifetime of being engulfed by her mom, change doesn't happen overnight, but Janice related that she had to come up with a straightforward phrase to prevent her mother from constantly telling her how to run her life:

I finally made a decision to be absolutely clear with my mom. I'd had it with her unwanted advice about how to handle my daughter, my job, my marriage, and even what I made for dinner. Throughout my childhood and teens, I put up with her bossiness because I didn't have it in me to stand up to her. But separating from her emotionally, not giving in to what she wants me to do, and trying to figure out what I want—it's a goal I'm taking seriously. So whenever she tries to get bossy with me, I make it real clear. I just say, "Remember, Mom, I'm a grown-ass woman now."

Isaac, forty-four, related what he had to do to remind his engulfing narcissistic father to back off. Like Janice, he found a way to confront his parent's inappropriate intrusiveness:

One day, we were working together cleaning the basement. I was getting fed up with him ordering me around to move this here and move this there. So I just stopped in the middle of the room and acted like I was pondering something. Dad yelled at me and asked me what the hell I was doing. I simply said, "Dad, I am standing here trying to figure out how old I am." My dad got it. Now all I have to do to get my message across is just stop in my tracks and act like I'm pondering, and he remembers this.

David, forty-eight, told me a very strange story about his engulfing narcissistic mother. As he began journaling about his past and how to psychologically separate from his mom, he remembered the many ways she had sent him the message that her needs and wants were more important than his—and that the boundary between them was paper thin.

My mother used to pack my lunches for school, and she usually made me some kind of sandwich. But each day when I opened my lunchbox at school, there would be a bite out of the sandwich. She always took the first bite! I used to think it was strange, and I kind of felt violated, but I just accepted it and never said anything. Now I realize it was just one of the ways she was always reminding me that she had control over me. My recovery helped me see this strange behavior as a violation and a lack of boundary between myself and my mother. I am working hard on allowing myself control over my own life and to accept that my mother won't ever really change.

Molly, thirty, was terrified of her ignoring father because of his ongoing narcissistic rages. As a child, he had essentially ignored her presence unless it was to reprimand her for something very minor. She was generally an obedient, shy child who yearned for his attention and love but never received it. He would still yell and swear at her as an adult, until she discovered that she had to come back at him in a similar way:

I only did this once, but the day I did it, I realized I was no longer afraid of my dad and could feel like a separate person. He was swearing at me and telling me how stupid I was about something I believed in and reminding me that he was always right. He was literally in my face yelling. I had had enough, so I forcefully said to him, "Dad, you know what? You are just full of shit! I no longer have to listen to you. I am an adult." Boy, was he surprised that I could be that blunt! But it worked.

Ely, forty-two, was basically ignored by his single, narcissistic mother. He tried many things to get her attention, love, and approval, but nothing really worked. He learned in recovery to give up the expectations and quit trying:

My dad left us when I was a baby, and I was raised by my self-absorbed mother. She was too young to have a child and really wanted to party and have fun with friends. I was left alone a lot, but even when she was home with me, it was like I wasn't even there. She was on the phone or doing other things and didn't interact much with me. It was so lonely. I tried to get her attention in a lot of ways. Sometimes doing something really nice for her and a lot of times being naughty just so she would notice me. Now as an adult, she barely knows anything about me, my career, my family, or anything. She rarely calls and never visits us. I had to learn to accept this and let go of all expectations that she was going to change. It still feels sad not to have a family, but I no longer feel that deep sadness and yearning. I've just accepted who she is, and I don't even try anymore with her.

Journal Topics and Questions on Breaking Free from Being Engulfed or Ignored

- Finish this sentence: I had an engulfing narcissistic parent, and it made me feel . . .
- Finish this sentence: I had an ignoring narcissistic parent, and it made me feel . . .
- Finish this sentence: I experienced both kinds of narcissistic parenting behavior and it confused me in this way . . .
- Write a letter to your narcissistic parent about their engulfing or ignoring behavior, telling them how it affected you. Don't send the letter. This is for therapeutic purposes only.

Summarizing Your Step 2—Separation and Individuation Work

Over the course of this chapter, you have engaged in recovery work that supports psychological separation from your narcissistic parent and an individuation process toward becoming a more self-realized, authentic you. This work included the following:

- Letting go of the role you played in your family
- Owning your uniqueness
- Opting out of triangulation
- Becoming aware of a narcissistic parent's projected feelings
- Overcoming a narcissistic parent's envy
- Talking back to internalized negative messages
- Challenging the family mantra
- Breaking free from being engulfed or ignored

Now that you have completed this work, take some time to review your journal entries for Step Two, after which you can summarize your thoughts and insights concerning your own separation and individuation story.

Journal Topics and Questions Summarizing Your Separation and Individuation Story

- What have been the biggest challenges in separating psychologically from my narcissistic parent and the narcissistic family dynamic?
- How have I succeeded in confronting those challenges? What am I still working on?
- In what ways have I become an individual, apart from the roles, beliefs, mantras, and emotional routines that I learned in my narcissistic family?
- What have I worked on in order to overcome the negative internalized messages I grew up with?
- What strategies have been most helpful in achieving a stronger sense of myself as an individual?

How Do I Know I Have Completed Step 2— Separation and Individuation?

When you have worked hard on Step Two, you will begin to notice these differences in yourself:

- You are now able to feel a full range of feelings, good and bad, and have learned to express them appropriately.
- The angst of self-doubt is lifting, and you are believing in yourself more and trusting your own feelings.
- You are no longer fearful of your narcissistic parent and what they think of you.
- You are defining your authentic self and giving yourself credit where credit is due.
- You are more comfortable being alone and finding meaning from within.
- Your inner core feels more authentic and solid.
- You are finding it easier to express yourself in your relationships.
- You can identify projection and envy when they present themselves.
- Your internal negative messages are not as intense.
- You are being more kind to yourself.

+ You are able to look at your family's dynamics in a more objective way and are not getting pulled into the sticky web of family dysfunction.
+ You are having fewer PTSD triggers or collapses.

Moving On ...

Now that you have worked on Steps One and Two, you are ready to move on to Step Three—Re-Parenting the Wounded Child Within and Becoming Who You Truly Are. It will focus on strengthening your internal parent and developing your sense of self.

Chapter Eleven

Step 3—Re-Parenting the Wounded Child Within and Becoming Who You Truly Are

I'm learning about self-acceptance and self-compassion. I've never been good at this. I used to be so codependent, always putting others' feelings above my own needs. It's so freeing to be able to actually work on developing me. I'm finding a me in there!

—Zoe, 32

Step Three is the transformative journey into self-discovery. We will begin with strengthening your internal parent and re-parenting the wounded child within and then move on to discovering and developing your sense of self. Emphasizing self-acceptance is crucial in order to help you master self-love and compassion. You'll be invited to explore your core values and beliefs, as well as the passions, talents, and natural gifts that make you who you are. Learning to allow yourself to experience joy is also an important part of Step Three.

Strengthening Your Internal Parent and Re-Parenting the Wounded Child Within

To do this work, you will be working with your maternal or paternal adult self and your internal child, using your strengths as an adult to re-parent the wounded part of you. You may find that, like many adult children of narcissistic parents, you'll initially have difficulty knowing how to be an empathic, nurturing parent because your own parents likely did not provide good role models. But if you have patience and try the various exercises in this chapter, I believe you will be able to become the loving parent that your wounded inner child needs you to be.

If you have trouble envisioning yourself as a parent to your inner child, think about how you treat children—either your own children or children you've known at various ages. And also think about how you *feel* about children. Begin by answering these questions:

+ Do you believe children have rights, wishes, needs, desires, thoughts, and dreams?
+ When children are hurting, do you want to help them?
+ Do you naturally want to be kind and compassionate with a child?
+ Do you naturally want to calm and comfort a child and help them to feel safe?

Most of you will answer yes to these questions. And the yes answers will form the basis for the strength you'll be using to soothe and nurture your inner wounded child. Give yourself credit for this loving and compassionate side of you as you engage with the various exercises in this chapter. You may want to journal about your loving and caring adult self as you proceed.

If any of the exercises in this chapter seem silly or inappropriate to you, feel free to skip that one and try another, as some activities work better than others, depending on the person.

Find Photos of Yourself as a Child

In order to make the image of your wounded child more concrete, find photos of yourself as a child. You can choose one or more of you at any age, but typically photos of yourself at around five or six years old are very helpful. You may also want to find photographs from different developmental stages and ages.

As you go through the photos of your childhood self, take special notice of your body language and the expression on your face. Do you look happy, sad, scared, lonely, or anxious? It is helpful to journal about what you see in yourself as you view these photos. Write down anything that strikes you. The photographs of you as a child will likely bring back memories, some of which may be upsetting or difficult in some way. Whatever comes up for you as you view these photos, write about your memories and the feelings they elicit.

One of my clients found a picture of her mother holding her on her lap, but not close to her chest. The mother had her arms extended so that she was actually holding her daughter away from her body. She looked very uncomfortable holding her child. Another client remarked that in a photo of him and his dad sitting on the couch, he had his arm around his father but his dad had his hands in his lap, apparently not wanting to touch his six-year-old son. One woman found a photo of her beautiful narcissistic mom smiling broadly as the young daughter stood expressionless by her side.

Once you have found your pictures, find frames for them. The frames should be meaningful to you and represent something you really like—a color, texture, or anything you find beautiful. For example, you might choose a frame in a color you love or one that is adorned with flowers, pets, artwork, sports, or musical instruments. I have a client who chose a frame decorated with pianos because she loves playing the piano and is soothed by piano music.

Once you have selected and framed your photographs, place them or hang them where you will see them often, and make sure you can move them to wherever you do your journal work. Your adult self will be talking to and writing to your wounded child, so you'll want to be able to look at a photograph of yourself as a child as you write.

Travis, forty-five, shared the significance for him in working with childhood photos of himself and his family:

I was stunned when I found a photo of myself as a little boy. I looked so sad. The photo really helped me to have empathy for that little kid, and it made me want to be more kind to myself as an adult. When I watched old family movies, I could see my narcissistic father wanting perfection in our videos and my mother yelling at him to stop. We kids just looked stunned and confused and definitely not laughing or playful. So, yes, these exercises helped me tune in to my inner kid. I just felt so sorry for him.

Claudia, fifty-five, discovered something interesting when she started looking through her cedar chest for old pictures of her childhood:

I found a picture of my narcissistic mom lying on a hospital bed, propped up and posing for the camera like a model. On the back of the picture, she had written me this note: "This is from the day you were born. I know I must have a picture of you as a baby somewhere!" This photo and what Mom wrote on it really helped me to empathize with myself. I realized how much I wanted to nurture my wounded child, because I don't think I was even a wanted child. It was all about my mom.

Begin to Talk to Your Child Within

Now that you have a visual sense of your child within, you can begin to talk to that child. Here are some suggestions for how to start the conversation:

- Ask the child how they feel.
- Tell the child you will be there for them and that you care about how they feel.
- Ask the child what they need from you now.
- Using your compassionate adult self, tell the child how you feel about them. Say as many nice things as you can think of to your inner child.
- Ask the child what is most soothing to them when they are upset.
- Reassure the child that you will give them what they need.

This exercise may feel a little strange at first, but that is normal. Be sure to write down what your inner child is telling you as you are tuning in to them. And don't be surprised if the wounded child initially reacts with anger due to the fact that you may not have been taking good care of them. As you are working on Step Three, continue to repeat this exercise, so that you are frequently tuning in to your wounded child and checking in on what they need from you.

Create a Gift Box for Your Inner Child

This special gift box for your inner child should be like the picture frames and represent something you really like.[23] The box can be any size. As you are working to re-parent your wounded child, you'll be giving the child gifts that will go into the box.

The gifts should mean something special to your child. Maybe it is a favorite candy, toy, or flower. It could be pictures of things you liked to do as a child, music you liked, or creative activities you enjoyed when you were young. One of my clients wrote poems to her child and put them in the special box. Another bought small replicas of cars and trucks he treasured as a child and put them in his box. And another found miniature animals to put in her child's box, representing her favorite pets. Gifting your inner child in this way will bring a smile to your face and bring you closer to that wounded young person.

Create a Parent Box for Unwanted Items

Some adult children I have worked with also like to create a parent box—for things that represent unpleasant or unwanted aspects of their narcissistic parent. If you choose to create a parent box, you can put in it images that depict things about your narcissistic parent that you no longer want in your life. Images may include pictures of food, clothing, or activities that your parent insisted on, but that you didn't like. You can also put into the box slips of paper on which you write down the unwanted punishments, sayings, or negative messages you got from your narcissistic parent.

Doll Therapy

Some clients groan when I mention this exercise, but lots of people have enjoyed it and found it emotionally therapeutic.

Buy a doll that appears to be about five or six years old. The doll should look something like you as a child, in terms of hair color, complexion, and style. And it's good if you can find a soft doll that you can hold and cuddle.

The doll becomes a very concrete representation of your child within, and you can rock it, hold it, talk to it, and love it. The doll can be placed on your bed, couch, dresser, or close to your computer, so you can also use the doll to talk to your inner child and ask what they need from you each day. Some male clients may want to use a cute teddy bear dressed in little boy clothes instead of a doll. Many of my male clients have skipped this exercise, but the ones who do it have fun. In fact, one man loved bringing the doll to therapy because he enjoyed sitting in our reception room with it while children also waiting in the room gave him questioning looks. We used to laugh about this. But in therapy he would hold the bear while we practiced talking to his inner child, and he found it very helpful.

Clarissa, forty-five, shared that she felt she had started to tune in to her wounded child even when she was still a child, but had not understood why she always played this repetitive game in the backyard until she engaged in doll therapy as an adult. She realized that she had been acting out her trauma in her play as a child.

> I used to take my doll and sit her under a tree and spread her arms out like she was reaching out for me. Then I would walk away and turn around and see her reaching for me, and I would race back to her and grab her up and hold her and rock her. I didn't understand what I was playing out until now. Doing the doll work has been especially helpful to me in learning how to nurture myself.

Clarissa was clearly acting out her desires as a child to be held, rocked, and loved. She was giving her childhood doll what she herself needed.

Visualize Yourself as a Child

Find a quiet, alone space where you can close your eyes and visualize yourself as a child at various ages. Bring up pictures in your mind of yourself as a kid. Then talk to that child as your adult self, making sure to be especially kind and compassionate with them. Listen to your childhood self and respond with understanding and love.

When I was working my own recovery, I used this visualization exercise, and it was very beneficial. I would sit in a rocking chair after my children were in bed, close my eyes, rock back and forth, and imagine myself as a little child. I would get a visual image of a little girl with long blond braids and red cowboy boots. I would then hold out my arms and ask her to come to me and tell me what she needed from me. At her first appearance, she was a sad, stomping, red-booted, angry kid, but as she talked to me, I became aware that I wasn't taking good care of her and needed to do that now. We talked a lot about what she missed as a child. I repeated this visualization exercise frequently and then journaled about each interaction.

Talk to Your Wounded Child About Changing Negative Messages to Positive Ones

We talked previously about internalized negative messages, and in Step Two you worked on identifying your most prominent ones. Now that you have a more concrete sense of your inner child, through childhood photos and your doll, it is time to start talking back to those negative messages in the presence of that child.

Using your paternal or maternal adult self, talk to your wounded child about those negative messages, telling them what the truth is behind the messages. Adult children of narcissists make erroneous assumptions about themselves because of what they have been taught. Adult children also tend to have unrealistic expectations of themselves. These expectations and incorrect assumptions need to be changed. So, for example, if your most prominent message is *I am not good enough*, talk to your inner child about *why you are good enough*. Change the negatives to positives using self-love and compassion.

The child within may fight this shift in perspective in the beginning, so you just have to keep reassuring your young self that it is okay to be who they are, and that they are good enough, worthy, and lovable. This does not mean that you're saying you never made mistakes in your life; we all do as we progress on our life's journey. But it is time to forgive yourself for your mistakes and remind your inner child that we are all human and make mistakes like everyone else.

To accomplish self-love and self-compassion, we need to start with self-acceptance. Self-acceptance means accepting yourself for the totality of who you are: your weaknesses and strengths, mistakes and accomplishments, passions and dreams. You only have to be good enough for you. Then you can practice giving yourself love and compassion. And you can do this by practicing with your childhood photograph and/or doll.

Through these exercises and practices, we can learn that our validation comes from within ourselves, rather than from external sources. We can be our own strong adult parent, who will always be with us and who will always keep loving and supporting our inner child.

Journal Topics and Questions on Re-Parenting the Wounded Child Within

The following are additional journaling activities to assist you with re-parenting the wounded child within. These exercises can help you to empower yourself and your inner child.

- Write to your wounded child about self-acceptance, self-forgiveness, self-love, and compassion. Identify what is working for you and what barriers still exist.
- As a way to tell your inner child who you are as an adult, make a list of *I am* statements in your journal. Begin each statement with *I am* . . . Start with simple statements and keep digging deeper until you have identified core aspects of your character. For example, you might begin with "I am Richard, I am forty-five. I am a father. I am a husband. I am a contractor. . . ." Then, move to your deeper character traits, such as "I am friendly. I am honest. I am a good friend. I am trustworthy. I am kind. I am loving. . . ."
- Using the voice of your maternal or paternal self, write in your journal to your wounded child, telling them that they are a loving and good person.
- Using your adult voice, write to your wounded child about what you like and treasure about their character and value system. For example, "I love how you are kind to others and respect others even if you disagree with them."

- Using your adult voice, write to your inner child telling them what you like about their body. Reassure that wounded child with compassion, understanding, kindness, and support. Don't fall into the trap of writing about the things you *don't* like, as we all have certain aspects of our physical bodies that we may not like.
- Write about what you have found to be soothing for your inner child. For example, remind yourself what is calming for you. It may be certain music, going for a run, meditating, breathing exercises, or doing puzzles.
- If you have family photo albums, movies, or videos in which you appear as a child, take some time with them and then write down your thoughts in your journal, expressing empathy for your inner child.

Searching for My Authentic Self

Now that you have learned how to better tune in to your wounded child and are practicing self-love and compassion, it is time to begin the search for the authentic you. This part of Step Three will suggest exercises to help you discover and develop your genuine self.

Create a Collage that Represents the Authentic You

Create a collage that represents significant things about you . . . what you believe, what you love, your dreams and passions, special talents and traits. The collage can include small items, fabrics, photographs, and images from the internet or magazines that reflect who you are. Combine these elements in your own creative way. Everything in the collage should signify something meaningful about your authentic self. In creating the collage, notice and think about who you really are on a deep level.

One of my male clients recently created his collage from images he found on the internet. Being a musician, he started with an image of a piano. Prominently featured was a picture of a woman and a child, representing his wife and daughter. He also included elements representing things he particularly liked, such as classic cars, Mexican food, gardening, stamp collecting, baseball caps, and open spaces in the countryside. The collage was lovely, and my client enjoyed doing it and telling me about it. The images he chose reflected what he loved, what he liked, his life values and character traits. I thought it was cute that he included a huge plate of donuts!

List What You Love to Do for Fun and in Your Free Time

Make two separate lists: one for what you like to do in your free time and the other for the things you love to do for "kick up your heels" fun. On the free time list, you might include such things as taking walks, reading, gardening, watching TV, working on your car, building things, knitting, playing an instrument. For the "kick up your heels" list, write down the things you do for fun that really jazz you, make you laugh, and take you away from your busy life and worries. On this list, you might list such things as: dancing, snowboarding, roller skating, throwing a party, or playing family games. These are the kinds of activities that make you laugh out loud and really have fun. This list is important because it will remind you how to bring joy back into your life.

Some adult children of narcissistic parents have trouble with this exercise. I hear comments like "I don't even know what I like to do," "I don't have any hobbies," and "All I do is work." If you have trouble listing things that you do for fun, think back to when you were a child. What kinds of toys did you like to play with? What activities were you naturally attracted to? One of my clients was struggling with this exercise until she started thinking of what she loved as a child. She remembered this:

> I used to love to listen to country music on the radio. This helped me figure out what would be super-fun to do as an adult and I started country dancing. It's the best. When I am twirling on the dance floor, all my worries go away.

Rediscover Your Talents and Passions

In searching for the authentic you, it's important to assess your special talents. Were you born musical or artistic or athletic? Were you especially attracted as a child to certain activities that utilized your special talents? We all have some things we are better at than others. Acknowledging what you're particularly good at doesn't mean you have to be a superstar, but doing this exercise will help you rediscover particular talents that you may have forgotten about. Sometimes we get so busy that we forget about the talents we developed earlier in our lives but which we are no longer expressing as adults. Your creative side needs expression. It's there for a purpose.

What about your passions? Not everyone has a passion, but it's never too late to cultivate one. Do you have an interest that you have never explored? Do you allow yourself to follow your curiosity? Now is the time to give yourself the reward of being passionate about something. You deserve it. If you don't have a particular passion yet, that's okay. What's important is to start tuning in to what interests you and allowing yourself permission to try new things. You may find something to be passionate about as you continue your recovery work and discover more about who you are.

Write in your journal about the special talents you once exhibited and would now like to get back to. Also, journal about new passions you would like to pursue.

Gail, fifty-eight, played the guitar in her twenties but rediscovered her passion for it later in life:

> *Music wasn't valued in my family, and my narcissistic dad's preferences always overrode what I might have wanted. But as soon as I left home after high school, I bought myself a used guitar and loved playing it. I recently found my old guitar in the back of a closet, got it re-strung, and decided to take a few lessons to brush up. I really got into it—and I love it! It's just for me, but whenever I'm in the mood I pick it up and love how it makes me forget everything else and just live in the moment for the music.*

Don, forty-nine, used to build model planes when he was a kid but had forgotten how much pleasure he had derived from that particular activity:

> *It seems like an odd thing for a grown man to get involved in, but I just decided—what the hell, it's fun! And I'm really good at it. I gave myself permission to enjoy something that I had loved when I was a kid.*

Inventory Your Physical Well-Being

How are your physical health and body image? As you work on your authentic self and becoming more self-compassionate, it is time to take an inventory of your physical well-being also. A big part of who you are includes your physical self. Are there health issues you've ignored and now need to focus on? Doctor appointments you need to make? Are there addictions you are trying to control or get rid of? Do you need to be doing more exercise in your daily life? What is your body image like? Do you want to work on changing it? Are you sleeping well enough? Is workaholism a concern? Are you controlling your stress level?

Take some time to write in your journal about your overall physical health and make a list of what you want to work on to improve it. Using your newfound maternal or paternal compassionate self, work on taking really good care of yourself. Your wounded child will thank you.

Assess Your Preferences, Values, and Beliefs

As we've learned throughout the book, children of narcissists are often obliged to keep their own preferences, values, and beliefs under wraps. As an adult, it is now time to allow yourself to discover what you truly desire, enjoy, value, and believe.

The following is a list of questions that should get you thinking about who you are: what you like, what you enjoy, what you're interested in, what you value, what you believe in. Hopefully, it will spark your own thoughts concerning what makes you *you*. After reviewing the questions, I encourage you to journal your answers, taking your time to answer a few questions every day. The questions range from fairly mundane interests and preferences to deeper philosophical values and beliefs. Respect your unique thoughts and ideas as you answer these questions. Your journal responses will give you a newly created self-portrait—one that reflects the authentic you.

Note: As you answer these questions in your journal, explain in as much detail as possible why you have answered them in the way that you have.

♦ What would be your choice of an ideal vacation?
♦ Where in the world would you most like to travel?

+ What are your favorite foods?
+ What sports do you enjoy playing?
+ What sports do you enjoy watching?
+ What kind of movies do you like to watch?
+ What type of books do you like to read?
+ Which clothing styles appeal to you?
+ Which season is your favorite?
+ What kind of music do you like to listen to?
+ What kind of dancing do you enjoy?
+ What kind of exercise do you most enjoy?
+ What topics of conversation do you most enjoy—and with whom do you enjoy having these conversations?
+ What are your beliefs regarding education—for yourself and for your family?
+ What are your political beliefs?
+ What are your religious and/or spiritual beliefs?
+ If you are a parent or plan to become one, what is your parenting philosophy and what are your priorities as a parent or potential parent?
+ What is most important to you in a love relationship?
+ What personal qualities would your ideal love partner possess?
+ What kind of friends are you attracted to?
+ What do you appreciate most in a friendship?
+ What brings you a sense of contentment?
+ What brings you a sense of personal fulfillment?
+ What brings you joy?

How Do I Know When I Have Completed Step 3—Re-Parenting the Wounded Child Within and Becoming Who You Truly Are?

When you have completed Step Three, you will begin to enjoy these self-affirming and life-affirming benefits:

+ You will feel tuned in to your inner wounded child.
+ You will be nurturing and listening to the needs and feelings of your wounded child.

+ You will be taking care of your wounded child.
+ You will be much more self-accepting, and able to give yourself more self-love and compassion.
+ You will not be beating yourself up over your mistakes.
+ You will have identified core elements that comprise your authentic self: your preferences, values, dreams, and desires.
+ You will find yourself doing more internal validation and needing less external validation.
+ You will find yourself able to do more self-soothing.
+ You will be defusing negative messages and replacing them with more positive messages that more accurately represent your true reality.
+ You will allow more creativity in your life.
+ You will allow more joy into your life.

The Giraffe Club

In the previous chapter, I mentioned the uniquely expansive qualities of a giraffe and how those traits represent our position in a narcissistic family. Rather than thinking of ourselves as the "black sheep" of our family, we can join the tribe of recovering adult children of narcissists in what I call *the Giraffe Club*. We are changing the description of ourselves from black sheep to far-sighted giraffes.

Imagine a grassy meadow with tall trees at the far edge. In the meadow is a flock of sheep, their heads down, all doing what the next guy does. But in the midst of this flock of sheep are giraffes. Long-legged and long-necked, they can see beyond the tops of the trees at the far end of the meadow. Above the trees are things the sheep can't see: sunrises, sunsets, visions, dreams, possibilities, problem-solving, and healing growth.

The sheep are constantly bleating to the giraffes to be quiet, to get down to their level and be like them. The flock of sheep, which represents our narcissistic families, tells us: don't stray from the flock, and don't challenge the status quo by telling us that there are problems in this family.

Giraffes clearly don't fit in with the sheep. Their vision is grounded, but they are also farsighted. They can see things sheep can't see. With their towering necks they can perceive a wider environment, a more all-encompassing truth. As metaphorical "giraffes" with a more authentic, far-reaching perspective, we can talk about *the elephant in the room*, meaning the dysfunction in our narcissistic families. The giraffe is a power animal that sees the truth of its environment, embraces healing, and represents the importance of believing in yourself.

Welcome to the Giraffe Club![24]

Moving On...

Now that you have worked on developing and strengthening your authentic self, and are celebrating and taking care of who you really are, you are ready to move on to Step Four—Managing Your Narcissistic Parent and the Rest of the Nest.

Chapter Twelve

Step 4—Managing Your Narcissistic Parent and the Rest of the Nest

It's all about setting boundaries now. It's hard to understand why it took me so long to be able to draw my line in the sand with my parents and family. I've learned that the way to make boundaries stick is to stick to them. They still think I am the "problem child," but I don't care anymore.

—Cherie, 42

Step Four is when you, as a newly recovering survivor, begin to make decisions about what your relationship with your narcissistic parent and the rest of your family is going to look like going forward. There is a big leap in healthy self-agency at this stage. Armed with an understanding of the emotional triggers you must manage, your ability to establish boundaries and limits will ensure that your recovery progresses. This may mean deciding that you will have no contact or low contact with one or more of your family members in order to enhance your well-being and foster a more manageable relationship with them.

In this important chapter, we will be discussing your decisions regarding contact with your family, the art of setting boundaries, the concept of forgiveness, dealing with your narcissistic parent as well as the other members of your family, additional grief issues, understanding family patterns of parenting and narcissism, and acknowledging the gifts you may have received growing up in your particular family.

Decisions About Contact with Your Family

In the beginning of recovery, the adult child of a narcissistic family often has to make a decision to have a temporary separation from their narcissistic parent and other family members in order to be able to work their recovery without getting triggered. We discussed the issue of contact earlier in the book, but as I always advise my clients, it is best not to make the final contact decision until you get to Step Four. This is because once you process the trauma, you may come to a different decision about whether or not—and to what degree—you should maintain contact with your narcissistic parent and other family members. At the beginning of your recovery, it may feel like no contact is the only choice, but after embracing the work, many people make a different decision. There are, however, very toxic and dangerous situations that require an immediate no contact, so the contact decision is very case by case.

No Contact

No contact means that you make the decision to completely cut off contact with your narcissistic parent and/or other members of your family, depending on the situation. You choose not to have any interaction with them. Often the no-contact choice applies differently to different members of the family; you may have some contact with some members and no contact with other members.

No contact is a big decision, and it usually creates more grieving and sadness, but in many cases, it is important for the sanity and mental health of the recovering person.

When adult children make the decision to have no contact with one or more family members, they may do so in a number of ways. Some stop seeing or communicating with the family member(s) gradually, so that they and the family become used to the break in communication. Others write a letter or email informing the person(s) that they are no longer interested in maintaining the connection.

My advice about informing your family members about your no-contact decision: if you decide to write something, keep it simple and to the point, without blaming anyone. Be sure to own it as *your* decision for *your* mental health. You do not have to defend, justify, or explain anything. Informing them of your decision is just a courtesy to let them know your intentions.

When you inform a narcissistic parent that you no longer intend to maintain contact, they will often up the ante and attempt multiple times to contact you. Some people have to block their parent on the phone or learn to ignore emails or texts. This is easier said than done. But if your mental health requires that you take the no-contact route, it is important that you do so.

Something to note here is that, depending on whether or not your narcissistic parent was engulfing or ignoring, they may react differently to your no-contact decision. The engulfing narcissist will be more likely to push the connection and try everything they can to sweep you back in. The ignoring narcissist may just let the relationship go and not even try to contact you, as they are more comfortable with ignoring you anyway.

Stacy, thirty-five, had an ignoring narcissistic mother and an enabling father. Remember that enabling parents often revolve around the narcissist; they're focused on the narcissistic parent, not the child. So when Stacy decided on no contact with her parents, neither of them seemed to notice.

> *I think my mother preferred having me out of the way, so she could keep my dad focused on only her. When I informed them that I was cutting off contact, she had nothing to say and didn't push the envelope. And my dad didn't say anything either. I knew it was the right thing to do for me, and it really proved the point of all I had learned in my recovery. They were in their own little world, and I didn't really count.*

Lloyd, fifty-six, had an engulfing narcissistic father. When he went no contact with his parents, all hell broke loose.

> *I told them I was no longer going to communicate and needed to be left alone. My dad hit the roof. He called, emailed, texted, and knocked on my front door multiple times. I felt like I was being stalked. My wife kept me sane as we went through this, and it finally settled down. But, before he quit,*

*my dad had some choice words to say about me, and of course he blamed it
all on my poor wife.*

Lloyd and his wife had to be on the same page with the no contact,
and they discussed their boundary setting over and over until it became
natural for them to do. Lloyd also repeatedly supported his wife when his
parents tried to blame her for everything.

Civil Connect

Civil connect is what I call having low contact but establishing a kind of
diplomatic relationship with your narcissistic parent and other family
members. When you make a decision to have civil connect, it means you
are maintaining contact, but less than you normally would. It also means
that you have accepted that you will not have an emotionally connected
relationship but rather one that will be quite superficial. You accept this
and proceed with your eyes wide open. You relinquish any expectations
of a deep or meaningful connection with your narcissistic parent or your
enabling parent. Their narcissistic and/or enabling attitude toward you
no longer hurts you to the degree it once did, and you decide that this
level of contact is the only way to keep at least some attachment to your
family.

You control this limited contact by enforcing boundaries. You don't
allow any abusive behavior and keep the contact with your family mem-
ber(s) very controlled. This means that when you want to remove yourself, you do. When you want to hang up the phone or stop texting, you
do. When you don't want to call or text someone back, you don't. You
learn to listen to the signals that your feelings are giving to your body and
do what is right for you. In civil connect, you keep the conversations and
interactions light and polite, and you make no attempt to be emotionally
close or vulnerable. Behaving in this way will keep you emotionally safe,
rather than at risk of being triggered. And with this level of contact at
this point in your recovery, you'll be much less likely to feel anxious and
disappointed.

As we discussed earlier in the book, civil connect does not really
work until you have worked through the trauma, worked on separation-

individuation, and embraced your recovery, so that you have no expectations with respect to developing a closer relationship with your parent or other members of your family.

If you choose to see members of your family, try to limit the time you spend with them. Don't bring up family dysfunction or problems in the family. Ask about how they're doing. You know they will like that! Don't bring up the work you're doing on yourself as they will likely be defensive and won't necessarily understand unless they are doing recovery also.

My client Merrilee, fifty-two, shared her civil connect experience with me:

I made a decision to do civil connect after working my recovery, but it took some practice. I called my parents about every two weeks just to check in on them. I knew the conversation would be all about them and that they would talk about what they had for dinner, what all the neighbors were doing, and would not ask about me or my family. I had no expectations that it would be different. I actually tried to tell them a joke each time, so I could keep it light. I learned not to be vulnerable and tell them about me, and of course, they didn't ask anyway.

In practicing civil connect with his family, Jerry, sixty-five, had an interesting observation:

When I decided to try civil connect, I thought it would be a big deal to them, but actually they didn't even notice. They were totally comfortable because they were used to being superficial and not deep anyway.

Journal Topics and Questions on Decisions About Contact with Your Family

♦ If you decided to go no contact, write about why you made that decision.
♦ Write a potential letter to your narcissistic parent or other family members that tells them of your no-contact decision. (You may or may not decide to send it. This letter is mostly for therapeutic purposes and helps you clearly define your decision and reasons for no contact.)
♦ Write about your fears concerning your no-contact decision.

+ If you decided to go civil connect, write about why you made that decision.
+ Write about your fears concerning your civil-connect decision.
+ Whether you decided on no contact or civil connect, write about your feelings of loss and grief regarding your decision.

Setting Boundaries

Setting a boundary means that you draw a line in the sand when it comes to interaction with the members of your narcissistic family. It means that you are absolutely clear about how you are going to behave with your family and are able to commit to these statements: "This is what I will do," and "This is what I will not do." The objective of setting boundaries with a narcissistic parent and other family members is to support your recovery and well-being.

The most difficult aspect of boundary setting is sticking to the boundaries when you're being harassed, pressured, or made to feel guilty. Many people have a difficult time setting boundaries because they don't want to hurt the other person's feelings, or they are afraid the boundary will cause the other person to not like them or to abandon them. If you fear abandonment, you are not alone. Most adult children of narcissistic families already feel emotionally abandoned and don't want to risk intensifying that sense of abandonment. But learning the art of setting boundaries is an important part of your mental health and taking good care of yourself.

Although setting boundaries with your family members can be done in a respectful manner, without justifying or defending your intentions, it can be difficult with a narcissist because they don't usually have or respect boundaries. And often the other family members were not taught to have or respect boundaries either, making it difficult for you to do so.

The need for boundaries can arise in numerous situations in the narcissistic family. Let's look at some examples and possible ways to deal with setting boundaries. The key is to state how you feel but not tell the other person what to do.

Your narcissistic mother says, "Honey, you have put on some weight. Do you want me to buy you some diet pills?"

You say, "No thank you. I am in charge of my own body and my own
weight, and I will decide what I plan to do and how I choose to look."

Your narcissistic father says, "I'm worried about your finances and how
you are being so irresponsible about money. How do you expect to
take care of your family?"

You say, "Look, Dad, I am an adult and I make my own decisions about
the money that I make. I don't appreciate your comments. In fact,
they are hurtful to me." ·

Your brother says, "Hey, Sis, why are you not coming to the holiday
breakfast with the family? I think that's totally rude to all of us.
Who do you think you are?"

You say, "I am busy with work and can't make it this year. I hope you have
a good time."

Your sister continues to take clothes out of your closet without asking to
borrow them and doesn't return them.

You say, "It is not okay with me that you take my clothes. It feels disre-
spectful and hurtful to me."

Your narcissistic parent says, "Every time I see your children, they look
like little bums. They are unkempt, and they embarrass me."

You say, "These are my children, and I will raise them as I see fit. Your
comments are hurtful to me."

Your narcissistic parent says, "Wow, this house looks like a tornado hit
it. Did you ever think of doing some cleaning or maybe hiring a
housekeeper?"

You say, "This is my house. I will handle my own housecleaning as I see
fit. Your comments are not helpful and are hurtful to me."

Notice the pattern of not telling others what to do, but clearly stating
your boundaries and, if you choose to, your feelings. Again, no need to
justify, explain, or defend.

If we don't set boundaries, we get run over emotionally and become
resentful and angry. But what if we set the boundary, and the other person doesn't respect it? When this is the case, it's time to move away from
the situation. Walk away, hang up the phone, leave the situation in whatever way you can. You don't have to get angry or cause a scene. You just
state the boundary, and if it's not respected, you are out of there.

Again, the key is to stick to the boundary you have set. Remember, you no longer allow any abusive behavior aimed at you. Abusive behavior automatically crosses a boundary by failing to respect a person's safety and well-being, and you do not put up with it. You simply remove yourself from the situation.

Here are some other examples of boundary-setting statements to add to your toolbox:

+ That is hurtful to me, and I am not going to listen to that right now.
+ I am sorry you feel a need to say that to me, but I am going to leave now.
+ That is an interesting comment. (Or just say: "Interesting!")
+ That is not okay with me.
+ I am not comfortable with that.
+ This does not work for me.

Darlene, forty-seven, struggled with setting boundaries with her narcissistic father but finally accomplished her goal. This is how she explained it to me:

I realized that I was very afraid of my dad. He would use rage to make me lose my nerve, and then make me feel so guilty if I didn't do everything his way. I really had to work on overcoming my fear. When I realized that he was not going to change, I started setting boundaries and felt a new sense of freedom. Now I just kindly state what I will do and what I won't do, and however he reacts, it is his problem, not mine.

Milton, forty-five, felt sorry for everyone except himself. He could always understand what was going on emotionally for other people and didn't want to make things worse by saying that he was no longer willing to act a certain way or do certain things. In other words, he couldn't bring himself to set healthy boundaries in his narcissistic family because he was stuck in his habitual role as a codependent caretaker. When we discussed this dynamic, Milton told me this:

I learned growing up that my needs didn't matter. I was there to take care of everyone else. My narcissistic mother made it clear to me that I had to take

care of my little brother and her and my enabling father. I was supposed
to be the strong one. Once I came to understand codependency and how
unhealthy it is, I realized that I could learn to set boundaries. I now stand
up for myself, and I feel like a different person.

As we have discussed throughout this book, we learn the wrong definition of love in a narcissistic family. For the child of a narcissistic parent, love means either *what I can do for you* or *what you can do for me*. This wrong definition becomes a setup for dependent and codependent relationships. We'll discuss this further in the next chapter, but it is important to know that when you stop the codependency and set boundaries, it may feel as if you are not being loving. That's because you learned the wrong definition of love in your narcissistic family.

Journal Topics and Questions on Setting Boundaries

♦ Write about the barriers to setting boundaries for yourself.
♦ Write about your fears about setting boundaries with your family.
♦ Write about your struggles with setting boundaries with your family.
♦ Write about who in your family has the most difficulty with boundaries—and why you think that is.
♦ Is there someone who tries to make you feel guilty if you set boundaries? Write about this.
♦ Do you know someone who has great boundaries? Write about why you respect them.
♦ Do you have a tendency to feel guilty when you set a boundary? Write about this.
♦ Write down your own boundary statements that have worked for you.
♦ Write about giving yourself credit for your new boundary skills.

How to Handle Forgiveness

How often do we hear that we have to forgive and forget? That if we don't practice forgiveness, it must mean we're bad people? On the other hand, some feel that forgiveness means letting an offender off the hook.

When abuse of any kind is involved, I see forgiveness as an inner letting go. It's not about letting someone off the hook; rather, it is a letting go of vengeful anger within you so that it doesn't eat you up inside. When you are able to let go in this way and forgive a narcissistic parent or other family member for the way you were treated, you are the one who feels better.

Lewis Smedes, professor of theology and ethics, and author of *Shame and Grace: Healing the Shame We Don't Deserve*, put it this way:

> The first and often the only person to be healed by forgiveness is the person who does the forgiveness. . . . When we genuinely forgive, we set a prisoner free and then discover that the prisoner we set free was us.[25]

While we may want to let go of our resentment and anger toward a narcissistic parent, forgiving a narcissist can be challenging because they are usually unaccountable for their abusive behavior. They don't believe there is anything wrong with the way they have parented and behaved toward you. If someone is genuinely sorry for their behavior, it is obviously easier to forgive them; but authentic remorse and accountability—a key to sound mental health—is something we don't often see in narcissists. So how do we get to forgiveness?

Although we're often told by friends and family that "the past is the past, get over it already," it's not that simple, especially when it relates to a traumatic childhood. We know that working through the trauma and doing our recovery work is the answer. And as we've learned throughout the last section of this book, it is a process. Once you're engaged in that process, I can assure you that the *letting go* kind of forgiveness will work for you. But you need to give it time to be authentic and effective.

As Lily, thirty-eight, told me:

> *In the beginning of recovery, there was no way I could just let it go. I felt so much anger toward my narcissist mom—and so much sadness, too. When people would tell me to just forgive her and let it go, I wanted to shriek at them that they did not understand. Now that I am this far in my recovery, I get it. Mastering my trauma was the key.*

Mastering the trauma, which Lily speaks of, means allowing yourself to work on your traumatic childhood by embracing your feelings and processing those feelings.

Shane, forty-three, came from a very religious background and was taught that forgiveness is the only righteous path. He came to therapy to work on issues that arose from being raised in a narcissistic family:

I was taught to forgive and forget. It is the way of the Church. Always take the high road. But what about how I feel? Was I supposed to just forget the way my father treated me throughout my life? I got stuck there and needed help. Learning about letting go internally has helped me to move on. It wasn't about making the abusive behavior okay. It was about not allowing it to control me any longer.

Some people struggle with forgiving themselves. In the early stages of recovery, you may have fought back, or acted out with your family members, not knowing how to handle the trauma associated with being an adult child from a narcissistic family. Maybe there were some things you said or did that you regret. Remember, it is okay to be human and okay to have regrets and to forgive yourself for things you didn't know how to deal with. This is a human journey.

Journal Topics and Questions on Handling Forgiveness

♦ Write about your struggle with forgiveness. What is your biggest barrier?
♦ Write about your personal values and how they relate to dealing with forgiveness. What were you taught about forgiveness?
♦ Write about forgiving yourself. This is very important to do, as we are all human. Before you understood your trauma, you may have reacted to it in ways you didn't like. Can you now forgive yourself?

Managing the Rest of the Nest

Given what you've learned about narcissistic family dynamics, there are decisions you'll want to consider regarding the other members of your family: the enabling parent and your siblings. How can you manage your relationships with these family members so that your recovery and healing proceed effectively?

The Enabling Parent

Although in some narcissistic families there are two narcissistic parents, the most common dynamic is one narcissistic parent and an enabling spouse parent who orbits around the narcissist. Sadly, both patterns result in neither parent's fulfilling the children's emotional needs. As an adult child of a narcissist and an enabler, you may find yourself in the position of having added trauma to work out regarding your enabling parent.

For example, why did this parent not protect you? Why did this parent always side with the narcissistic parent? The enabling parent was a part of a team of parents who were unable to meet your needs. What recovery work will you have to engage in in order to manage your relationship with your enabling parent? This recovery work may involve doing family therapy with your enabling parent if they are agreeable to that. If they are not, which is often the case, you may find you have to work the steps again with the focus on the enabling parent and how they hurt you by not protecting and standing up for you.

While some adult children have a close relationship with the enabling parent, others don't because the narcissist parent would have felt too threatened, and therefore they discouraged it. Whatever the particular situation in your family, it will be important to your recovery to figure out how to make peace in your heart with the enabling parent. You may have to make the same kind of decision about contact or no contact with this parent. Or the decision might be made for you by the narcissist, as was the case with my client, Jasmine.

Jasmine, twenty-nine, had a narcissistic mother and an enabling father. As an adult, Jasmine had some relationship with her father, but her mother was the ignoring type and there was basically no connection between the two of them. Jasmine and her family were planning a vacation trip that was fairly close to where her parents lived. She wanted her young son to be able to see his grandpa, even though Jasmine was not planning on seeing her mother.

I wanted to see my dad and I wanted my son to see his grandpa. I invited my dad to come join us for a lunch and some time together, but I did not invite my mom. Dad couldn't handle it, and I knew why. He was afraid of her wrath. He couldn't stand up to her. So he declined to come, and now we are back to basically little to no contact with him. It leaves me feeling so sad, but I am learning to accept it and know that this is how it will be. I cannot control this.

Robert, forty-five, was struggling to keep a connection with his mother, who was enabling to his narcissistic father. The mother and everyone in the family were afraid of the father's rage and his controlling behavior when things didn't go his way. Robert finally got the nerve to talk to his mom about this, and they found a way to maintain some level of connection. This is what he told me:

It was scary for me to bring this up with Mom, but I finally told her that I was probably not going to be communicating anymore with Dad, but I still wanted a connection with her. She agreed that we could talk, text, and email when Dad was at work or out of town. She didn't really like this, but she wanted to stay in touch with me, too. We both felt very sad about this whole thing. But it is working out okay. It's better than losing touch with her altogether.

Siblings

We've discussed how the children in a narcissistic family tend to be cast in roles such as scapegoat, lost child, and golden child. These roles may change over time, and one child may end up having all the roles eventually. It depends on what is going on in terms of the parental needs, which always take precedence over the children's needs.

If you have siblings whom you are close to, you are one of the lucky ones. I encourage you to share and process your family history with your willing sibling(s) if you can. If you join in the recovery process together, you can discuss your thoughts and journaling with each other. Having a sibling you can talk to about your family dynamic can be very validating and helpful to your recovery process.

Unfortunately, as I have found in my research and clinical practice, very often siblings raised in a narcissistic family are not close as adults. This is usually due to the fact that they grew up in a family in which they were not encouraged to be emotionally close or supportive of each other. Rather, they were likely faced with comparisons, competition, jealousy, and lack of mutual support.

If you are not close to your siblings, it can be another significant loss to deal with. I have seen many adult children in recovery who try hard to connect with their siblings but are disappointed in their efforts. Often the sibling isn't interested in recovery, may be threatened by the revelations of dysfunction in the family, may want to remain in denial, or is angry that their sister or brother is damaging the image of their "perfect" family.

If you learned codependency in your narcissistic family, which most of us did, you may be the one who tries to "fix" the family and bring them all together again, but to no avail. Your efforts may result in even more disappointment and that feeling of not being good enough. Reminder: un-learning codependency will have the positive effect of learning how to take care of yourself instead of focusing on taking care of the other person. While it's understandable that you would want a closer relationship with your sibling(s), what's most important is your healthy relationship to yourself.

Janelle, sixty, is close to her sister, and they can process family dynamics together. But she has two brothers who are very threatened by the sisters' bringing up anything negative about the family. Janelle explained:

I'm so grateful I can talk to my sister, but our brothers won't hardly speak to us, and we have very little connection with them. They just call us the "crazy" ones. It is very disturbing and sad to us because we are missing out on our nieces and nephews and extended family connections that we all need.

Janelle and I talked about learning to accept the limitations of her brothers but also trying to have individual connections with other extended family members such as her nieces and nephews.

Carl, fifty-two, has one brother and was raised in a family with a narcissistic father and enabling mother. The boys were pitted against each other, one the scapegoat and one the golden child. They were constantly compared, ended up being very competitive, and remain so to this day. Carl, the scapegoat, told me this:

> *I can see the dysfunction now and I don't blame my brother, but I also can't seem to forge a closeness with him. He seems to have taken on some of our dad's narcissistic traits and sees me as the "failure" of the family. He and my parents push me out and don't accept me as I am. Thankfully, I can now accept myself, but the losses are immense for me. I have this feeling of not being accepted and not fitting in.*

Carl had to go back to Step One to work on *acceptance* with respect to his brother's limitations. Although he had worked on accepting his parents' limitations, he needed to similarly work on accepting his brother's.

Growing up in a family led by a narcissistic parent affects everyone in your family. Therapeutically dealing with the consequences of having been raised in such a family involves managing the relationships you have with every member of that family. Your concerted effort in doing this work is an important part of your recovery, and the following journaling exercises will help you in this process.

Journal Topics and Questions on Managing the Rest of the Nest

- Write about your enabling parent and the kind of relationship you would like to have with them.
- Write a letter to your enabling parent telling them what hurt you in their parenting of you. (This letter is for therapeutic purposes, not to be sent.)
- Write about each of your siblings, focusing on their ability to see the dysfunction in the family.
- Write about the losses and grief that you feel concerning your enabling parent and your siblings.
- If you are an only child, write about how that affects your recovery as an adult child from a narcissistic family.

♦ Write about what you can change and what you cannot change in your
  relationships with members of your family of origin.
♦ Write about what you may need to accept about your relationships with
  members of your family of origin in order to move forward in recovery.

Understanding Your Extended Family's History of Parenting and Narcissism

Consciously or unconsciously, people often tend to parent their children
in the way that they were parented. They may not think about developing
their own parenting values or consider the effects of how they are treating their children. For example, if you were raised by an authoritarian
narcissistic parent, it may be a natural reaction for you to parent in the
same way, using stern behavior, shaming, and punishment rather than
empathy, teaching, and kindness.

So can narcissistic parenting be inherited by those whose parents were
narcissists? Indeed, narcissism can be passed down through the generations, because it is often misunderstood and improperly treated. With
that said, most adult children of narcissists tell me that they learned from
growing up in a narcissistic family what they did *not* want to do as a
parent.

Acknowledging and understanding your family's history of parenting
and narcissism can be helpful to your recovery. Where did your parent's
narcissism originate? Were they raised by narcissists and were their parents raised by narcissists? Sometimes narcissistic parents will talk about
their experiences growing up and what their parents were like, and this
can give you a clue as to the presence of narcissism in the family system.
But often they won't want to discuss their childhood, due to the pattern
of denial that is present in their family system. Still, it can be important
for your recovery to try to learn about your family's past history as it
relates to parenting in general and narcissism in particular. If you're
unable to uncover this information from your parents, you may be able
to find an aunt or uncle, grandparent, or close friend of the family who
will talk with you about previous patterns of behavior in your family and
extended family.

While it is true that societal values and parenting expectations change from generation to generation, and philosophies and belief systems may differ, I have not found that any generation in my lifetime is more narcissistic than the next. This is because narcissism is a personality disorder that exists within an individual, not necessarily within a culture. This distinction is best understood by looking back generations in your own family. You'll likely find relatives in your family system who knew how to offer empathy and emotional connection no matter what generation they came from and regardless of the societal values of the time.

For example, my grandmother, who was born in 1901, was a parent during the Depression and World War II, at a time when *children were to be seen and not heard.* And yet she was the most loving, nurturing, empathic person in my life. Her generation was all about hard work and grit, but she was loving, playful, and warm in her interactions with all people, especially children.

What might you discover about your own family's parenting history and the possible prevalence of narcissism?

Journal Topics and Questions on Your Extended Family's History of Parenting and Narcissism

- Is there someone in your family (outside of your immediate family) with whom you can discuss the extended family history? Identify those people and jot them down in your journal.
- Initiate conversations with these family members about the history of parenting in your extended family. Keep notes in your recovery journal.
- Ask relatives or family friends you trust to describe how they saw you as a small child, how they viewed your parents' parenting style, and what they know about your grandparents.
- If extended family members are unfamiliar with the meaning of narcissism, you can use these questions to start a conversation with them about your extended family:
    - Did you have a happy childhood?
    - Did you feel loved by your parents?
    - Did you feel you got enough attention growing up?

- Did your parents talk to you about feelings?
- Were you listened to, and did you feel heard?
- How were you disciplined when your parents were upset with you?
- Were you encouraged as an individual or did you have to fit the family image of what was expected?
- Was your mother or father particularly concerned about what others thought, instead of how you felt?

Did You Receive Any (Nonmaterial) Gifts Growing Up in a Narcissistic Family?

You'll probably be shaking your head no in response to the above question, saying, "I only received the knowledge that I don't want to be anything like my parents!" But people and situations are not necessarily black-and-white, and experiences are not always so clearly positive or negative.

At this point in your recovery work, it's time to think about what nonmaterial gifts you may have received while growing up in your family. Consider your parents' particular talents, abilities, and strengths—and how those may have been passed on to you.

For example, I was struck by a swarm of thoughts and memories after my mother died. I thought about her many talents. She was an amazing cook, baker, gardener, piano and organ player, musician, and vocalist—and she could rock and roll with that jitterbug. She could wallpaper anything, sew anything, knit, crochet, and needlepoint. She loved crafts. She was an exceptionally hard worker, very organized, and a very good housekeeper. I got some, but not all, of these amazing talents.

From my father, I think he passed down a great work ethic, self-discipline, and the love of dancing. He was also an avid collector and appreciated sentimentality in those collections.

I grew up in a narcissistic family, but I nonetheless received gifts from both of my parents.

You may have inherited your parent's curiosity and intelligence, or their musical, artistic, mechanical, or building ability. It's interesting and inspiring to think about positive attributes that have passed through the generations.

Although, as children from narcissistic families, we have to fully acknowledge and embrace the lack of emotional connectivity, empathy, nurturing attention, and unconditional love in our families, we can also be grateful for what we may have gained as family members.

Journal Topics and Questions on Acknowledging the Gifts You Received in Your Narcissistic Family

+ Take an inventory of your parents' talents, abilities, and attributes, and write them down in your journal.
+ Assess which of these talents, abilities, and attributes you possess, and write about them.
+ Write a letter of gratitude to your parents (that you don't send) for the gifts you received as their child.

Moving On . . .

Now that you have worked on how you will manage your family members in recovery, you are ready for Step Five—Ending the Legacy of Distorted Love.

You have come a long way. . . . Good for you!

Chapter Thirteen

Step 5—Ending the Legacy of Distorted Love

The most important part of Step Five for me was realizing that I was unconsciously attracted to the familiar and therefore seemed to pull in narcissists as friends and lovers. It was like I had a neon sign on my head that said, "I love narcissists!" Now I see the red flags and run.

—Dan, 37

The focus of Step Five is on helping you—a survivor of a narcissistic family upbringing—to cultivate self-awareness so that you don't repeat unhealthy relationship dynamics in your current life. When you're in recovery, you get to choose how you will relate to others, including your romantic partners, your friends, and your children. This step may entail ending relationships or severely curtailing interactions with unrecovered people, which may bring on more grief. But this grief, when processed, gives way to limitless possibilities, including the opportunity for true, unrestrained joy and happiness.

In this chapter, you'll learn about empathic parenting skills, healthy interdependent love relationships, and reciprocal friendships. I'll also provide the tools you'll need to monitor your own narcissistic tendencies so that they're held in check or eliminated entirely.

We can prevent a legacy of distorted love, and our recovery is the key. No more narcissism in the generations to come, if we have anything to do with it!

Since our own stories began with being the children of narcissistic parents, let's begin the untangling process by learning to become good parents.

Empathic Parenting

Most adult children of narcissistic families will tell you that they have a deep-rooted fear of turning out like their narcissistic parents. But the antithesis of narcissism is empathy. So if we want to prevent the legacy of narcissistic parenting, our first focus, if we have children or may have them one day, is to learn how to raise them with empathic parenting.

What is empathic parenting? Empathic parenting means that whenever troubling issues arise, we do our best to understand and validate our child's feelings before taking action. This is the core rule of empathic parenting, and it applies in nearly all situations. The exception would be if the child is in danger and we have to act quickly to protect them. For example, if a young child is running into the street, you must first stop them—and then employ empathic parenting. But in most cases, empathy and validation come first.

If you think about how you were parented within a narcissistic family, you'll likely realize that you were neither seen nor heard. You were probably taught to just follow your parent's rules. Your feelings didn't matter, so you didn't feel comfortable expressing them. In empathic parenting, it's all about the feelings. Empathic parenting means caring about how the child feels and acknowledging those feelings, so that they know their feelings are real. This doesn't mean giving in to a child's every whim. Rather, the child is always seen, heard, and understood, while also being taught to follow rules and do the right thing. As the parent, you're still the boss, because children don't feel safe unless they feel that their parent is in charge. But you're not in charge of your child's feelings; they are entitled to feel what they feel.

Let's look at the basics of empathic parenting, broken down into these five steps:

1. Help your child identify their feelings.
2. Repeat your child's expressed feelings back to them to make sure you've understood correctly what they're feeling.

3. Validate and empathize with the child's feelings.
4. Ignore the context of what brought on these feelings until steps 1 to 3 are accomplished.
5. Finally, deal with what initiated the child's feelings and what can be done about the situation.

How do we begin to help children identify their feelings? If you grew up in a narcissistic family, you might have missed this tutorial, so you may have to practice identifying your own feelings as you teach your child to do the same. Remember, adult children of narcissistic families were taught that their feelings don't matter, so as a parent you will be using new skills to teach your child that their feelings *do* matter.

To best understand how children learn about feelings, let's first consider very young children. At a very young age, children don't quite understand their feelings or know how to express them, until we teach them. Young children commonly act out their feelings by engaging in such things as hitting, kicking, crying, whining, pouting, or throwing things. You might be thinking, *That's actually similar to the way my narcissistic parent acted!* True, and that's because the narcissist gets stuck emotionally at a very young age. It's why they often act like six-year-olds.

Here is an example of how three-year-old Piper handles her feelings during a playdate with her friend Amanda, also three years old. Lucky Piper just got a new dolly for Christmas from her Nana, and she treasures it. But guess what Amanda wants to do? Amanda wants to play with that dolly, too. So she walks over and picks up the doll and begins to rock it. Piper is in shock. She is thinking, *That's my doll!* so she goes over to Amanda, pushes her, grabs the doll, and then starts to cry. Piper is very upset about Amanda taking her doll, but she doesn't know how to identify or deal with her upset feelings.

If Piper's parent had a non-empathic response, they might scold her for not sharing the doll, make her give the doll back to Amanda, and might even punish Piper by telling her she can't play with the doll anymore today. If they follow this course of action, Piper will have no idea what is going on and will be completely confused. She will likely think that she is a bad girl but will not know why. After all, she's probably thinking, *That's my doll! Amanda's not supposed to take my doll!*

If Piper's parent has an empathic response, however, they will follow the five rules listed above to handle this situation:

1. First, the empathic parent gets down to Piper's eye level and asks her what she is feeling. If Piper can't identify the feeling, the empathic parent will give her some ideas. For example, they might say: "Honey, what is wrong? Why are you upset?" Piper may or may not be able to identify her feelings as confusion and anger, even though she knows she's mad at Amanda for taking her doll.

2. If Piper can't identify her feelings, the empathic parent can say, "Honey, I bet you are feeling mad that Amanda wants to play with your doll." Piper may then say yes and keep crying.

3. and 4. The empathic parent then shows empathy for and validation of Piper's feelings, saying something like "I understand, sweetheart, that you are having trouble with Amanda wanting to play with your special doll. It's hard to share your special toys. I used to feel that way, too, when I was little. It is okay to have feelings and it is okay to be mad. We all get mad at times. Let's talk about being mad." Then Piper has a chance to express her important feelings, to feel heard and seen, and the empathic parent can validate those feelings. Once this is done, the child will typically settle down and it will be easier to move to the next step.

5. The empathic parent can now discuss sharing toys and help the two little girls with the sharing of the doll or whatever other solution the parent comes up with. Maybe Amanda can talk about her special toys, too.

The most important part here is to allow the child to have feelings, and to normalize and validate those feelings before working on a solution. Those of you who have been practicing this process already know that treating a child's feelings with this type of empathic attention will alleviate most tantrums and slowly teach the child how to identify and process their own feelings. They then learn that having feelings is okay and that talking about them is a good thing to do.

With young children, we start with just the basic feelings that they can relate to: mad, sad, glad, and scared. You can plug these feelings into many situations that a young child will be in. When I was treating young children in therapy, we would draw faces of mad, sad, glad, and scared, and talk about each feeling. You can also find *feelings charts* on the internet for almost any age group and post these on the refrigerator or someplace convenient in the house. You might want to look for an adult feelings chart, too!

The process of identifying and discussing feelings can be done with children of all ages. Let's take the elementary-age example of third grader Barry. Unbeknownst to his parents, Barry is being bullied at school by one of his classmates. One day, Barry wakes up and announces he is not going to school. He says he hates school and has a stomachache. This is new information to Barry's parents because up until now, Barry loved school and was an exceptional student.

A non-empathic parent would launch into a lecture about how important school is and announce that since Barry doesn't have a fever, he is "going to school. End of discussion!"

The empathic parent would follow the five steps.

1. and 2.   First determining Barry is indeed sick, the parents ask him about his feelings and what is going on. Usually when asked, children at Barry's age will tell you what they're going through and what they're feeling if they know you will listen. In fact, they need you to be there for them, to listen and understand them. When Barry tells his parents about the bullying that's been going on at school, they help him to identify his feelings of being upset and scared.

3. and 4.   Barry's parents validate his feelings and empathize with him. His dad might say something like "I understand how you must feel scared to be at school when your classmate is teasing and threatening you."

5.   Next, the parents move on to how to address the bullying problem. They don't make it about Barry being a bad kid for not wanting to go to school.

This 5-step process for dealing with a child's feelings can also be followed with teenagers. For example, Olivia, fifteen, wants to go to a party with her friends on a Saturday night, but her parents don't want her to go because they don't know the person who is hosting the party. They tell her she can't go. Olivia begins to throw a fit, calling her parents names and saying she hates them, while slamming her bedroom door.

The non-empathic parent is outraged at Olivia's behavior and yells at her while immediately imposing a punishment. "How dare you talk to your parents like that! No phone for you, young lady, for at least a week!"

The empathic parents calmly follow the five steps, tuning in to and identifying Olivia's feelings first.

1., 2., 3., and 4.   When Olivia expresses her anger at her parents for not allowing her to do what her friends are allowed to do, and her unhappiness about being left out of her peer group, her parents validate that her feelings are perfectly normal, and they empathize with her need to be with her friends.

5.   Validation will allow Olivia to help settle down, and begin to listen to reason and solutions. Her parents maintain their rules about needing to know whose home she will be spending time in, but they help Olivia come up with ideas about how she can be with her friends at another time soon. They talk to their daughter about being respectful, but they don't punish her for having intense feelings. They realize that helping Olivia manage her feelings is way more important.

While these examples of how empathic parenting focuses on a child's feelings rather than harsh punishment may seem commonplace, I have heard many disheartening stories from adult children about how they were severely punished by their narcissistic parents for displaying intense feelings. In such families, it is not okay for children to burden their parents with troubled feelings, so children's feelings are not acknowledged or respected.

The beauty of the five empathic rules is that they can be used in all types of relationships with all ages. These rules are also taught in couples therapy, so that couples learn to listen to each other, share their vulnerability, identify feelings, and learn validation and empathy with each other.

Key Parenting Values

In addition to empathic parenting, there are a number of other key parenting values that will help you prevent a legacy of tangled love in your family.

Show Your Children That You Value Yourself—and Them —Just as You All Are

If you grew up with a narcissistic parent and internalized the *not good enough* message, learning to value yourself and your children for who you are and who they are is perhaps the most important reason for your recovery work. Our children learn so much from what they see in us, versus what we tell them. Being aware of how important it is to model self-acceptance and self-love will help you to monitor when you may be acting out your own negative internalized messages from your past. Make sure that your children always know they are loved and accepted for who they are, just as you love and accept yourself.

Value the Person, Not Merely the Accomplishments

This is closely related to the previous key parenting value. It is so easy for us to focus on "my kid the soccer player" or "my kid the ballet dancer," but remember to primarily value and credit your child for who they are as a person. Look for the traits that reveal their character: how they treat other people, what they find to be most interesting and important, their curiosity, how they handle disappointment. One special friend of mine with a nine-year-old is always telling me sweet things about her son. These behaviors usually reflect his kindness, his sensitivity, how he cares about others, how curious he is about life, and what a good person he is. The child is also very accomplished in many things, particularly athletics, but his mother notices it all. Loving your child—or anyone else—is about loving who they are, not what they do.

Teach and Model Accountability

We've discussed the concept of accountability throughout the book, particularly in regard to the narcissist, who has little interest in it. So it makes sense that we want to teach our children how to be accountable for their behavior. The key here is to do this teaching without blame or shame. Learning to be accountable is a key to strong mental health. If we approach parenting with the understanding that everyone makes mistakes, and no one is perfect, and if we can teach children to own their behavior, we are on top of the game. It's also very important to model accountability for your children by acknowledging mistakes you make in your own life. For example, maybe you lose your cool sometimes and yell at your child as most parents have done. When you tell your child that you're sorry and wish you had handled the situation differently, they learn how to be accountable themselves.

Avoid Teaching Entitlement

Entitlement is a trait of the narcissist. While we want to treasure and cherish and unconditionally love our children, we don't want to give them the message that they are more important than others or that they deserve more than others. We all must learn to take our turn. We all have to stand in lines. We don't always win. We don't always get our way. It's great to give your child credit for the wonderful things they do and the sweet behavior they have, but that doesn't mean we should send them the message that they are better than others and therefore deserve more than others in life. This perspective can be modeled in a healthy way by verbalizing to our children that when we don't get what we want or when things don't go our way, we all have to accept that disappointment is sometimes part of life.

Develop and Apply Your Core Values

Remember in your recovery work, how you had to work on developing your core values? Applying those values is very important in parenting. If you are well aware of what you deeply value, you can parent in ways that meaningfully employ those values in your children's lives. For example, let's say you highly value the trait of kindness. You can model kindness in how you treat your family, friends, and others, so that your child sees an example of kindness in your behavior. And you can help your child practice treating others with kindness in their everyday interactions. Or perhaps you highly value a good work ethic. You can not only embody a healthy work ethic in your own life, so that your child is exposed to your conscientious behavior, you can also help your child develop a good work ethic by lovingly encouraging them to complete chores and homework in a manner that works for them.

Be Authentic

Being authentic means embodying our core values, being vulnerable, and sharing our real feelings and true self with others we love, including our children. Rather than putting on the image of the perfect parent or perfect person, being authentic with your child is about having the courage to be yourself. This commitment to authenticity also means that you allow your child to have intense feelings and to express them in appropriate ways. Your child doesn't always have to be happy or mild mannered. It's okay for them to be upset or sad or grumpy; just like us, they're only human. You can set the tone for them to talk openly about their less than happy feelings. When you're having a bad day, you can model for them how *you* can talk about your feelings. Children can sense when a parent is being inauthentic, but they can also learn from our authenticity that it's okay to be real.

Establish a Parental Hierarchy

We can lovingly and empathically parent our children and at the same time establish a parental hierarchy. Children feel safe when they know that you are clearly in charge and that it is your job to take care of them. You are there to guide, direct, teach, nurture, and love your children. It is not their job to do that for you.

As I have mentioned throughout this book, in the narcissistic family, the parent's needs take precedence over the child's needs. When you commit to preventing a legacy of narcissism, your child's needs take precedence. With that said, as the parent it is up to you to set boundaries and rules and expect them to be followed. You remain consistent and predictable. When this loving parental hierarchy is in place, your child learns to trust you, count on you, and lean on you.

Keep Your Door Open

We all make mistakes as parents. It's a tough job! Always keep the door open for your children to be able to talk to you about whatever they're going through. This applies whether your child is three years old or thirty. You simply tell your children that they can bring family issues to you and discuss their concerns, and that is okay with you. You can't go back and fix the past, but together you can work it through and heal in the moment.

Journal Topics and Questions on Parenting Values That Prevent a Tangled Legacy

- ◆ Go online to find *feelings charts* that you can use with your children at various ages. These charts are comprised of faces depicting various feelings, such as "sad," "angry," and "scared." The child can then point to the face that represents how they are feeling, and you can encourage them to express those feelings.
- ◆ Write about meltdowns your child has had and how the situation might have gone differently if you had followed the empathic parenting rules. Include what you wish you had said.
- ◆ Write about your experiences using the empathic parenting rules.
- ◆ Write about how you are modeling accountability.
- ◆ Write about how you are teaching your child that others are as important as they are.
- ◆ Write about the most important values you want to teach your child.
- ◆ Write about how you value your child's character, not merely their accomplishments.
- ◆ Write about how you're teaching your child about authenticity.
- ◆ Write about any struggles you're having in maintaining a consistent parental hierarchy.
- ◆ Write about the wonderful traits that you love about each child you have.
- ◆ Write about how you are teaching your child empathy.

Love Relationships

While much has been written about healthy versus unhealthy love relationships, this section will focus particularly on what adult children from narcissistic families need to watch out for, so that you don't fall for a narcissist.

In my clinical experience, I've found that, without recovery, we can be attracted to a familiar dynamic—one we likely grew up with in our family of origin. If you grew up in a narcissistic family, you may find that narcissists seem to find you, or you find them. It can be devastating to realize that after growing up in a family that embodies an unhealthy narcissism dynamic, you are now faced with a similar dynamic in your romantic relationship.

I can't tell you how many people I've worked with, interviewed, or who have emailed me who were raised in a narcissistic family and then became involved in a love relationship with a narcissist. This pattern is so prevalent that I wrote my second book (*Will I Ever Be Free of You?*) on this very topic.

Many adult children of narcissists feel ashamed about their failed relationships, but there is no need for shame. If the narcissistic dynamic—a distorted sense of love—was all you knew in your family, and if you didn't have a model of healthy relationships to follow, you can't blame yourself for what you didn't know. What is needed is recovery, so that you don't end up in a love relationship with a narcissist. Unfortunately, it is very common for adult children of narcissists to have a narcissistic partner. If this didn't happen to you, count yourself lucky.

The following qualities are aspects of a healthy love relationship that were too often missing in our narcissistic families but that we can now cultivate.

Interdependence

If you grew up in a narcissistic family, you learned the wrong definition of love. You learned that love is about what you can do for me or what I can do for you. Having learned this tangled notion of love means that you are likely set up for either a dependent or codependent relationship. The dependent individual is the one who leans on the other person and is the taker. The codependent individual is the caretaker and the giver. Neither role is healthy, and both roles can lead to unsatisfying, troubled love relationships.

A healthy relationship is interdependent, meaning there is an equal give-and-take between partners. At times you are the giver who is there for your partner when they need you, and at other times you may be the one who needs to lean on your partner emotionally or practically. In an interdependent relationship, partners are both caregivers and receivers of each other's care. They share in the giving and receiving of love and attention and support.

Amelia, sixty, had a series of failed relationships and came to therapy to try to figure out why her romantic entanglements always involved the same kind of partner and always ended badly. Her shame about choosing the wrong partners was palpable, and she had basically given up trying to get involved with anyone again for fear of repeating her past mistakes:

> *I feel so dumb. I keep choosing partners that I have to take care of. They mostly take advantage of me financially, and at first, I guess I'm okay with that, but eventually I become very resentful. I've learned that my fear of abandonment keeps me in a state of codependency with guys that don't treat me right. But I end up being abandoned anyway, because I keep choosing people who can't really love me.*

Amelia had to work on understanding how her codependency was related to her upbringing in her narcissistic family. She realized in her therapy that she was only valued by her narcissistic mother when she did everything the mother wanted her to do. She had to clean the house perfectly, become involved in activities her mother was interested in, and even dress like her mother wanted her to. She was valued if she acted in ways that would make her mother look good. This taught Amelia to be a caregiver to the exclusion of taking good care of herself and valuing herself.

Nick, fifty, was quiet, unassuming, flexible, and cooperative in his relationships, but he had a tendency to be overly dependent on his partners. He grew up in a family in which his narcissistic father demanded that he behave a certain way, look a certain way, and follow his directives as to what path he should take in everything from school subjects, to athletics, friendships, and career. Although Nick enjoyed success in his career and had lived on his own for decades, his early experience of having to constantly please his dad impacted his love relationships:

> *In therapy, I learned I had a pattern of being dependent on my partners and just letting them run the show. Things would be all right for a while, but*

then I'd feel like I had lost my sense of self. I never felt that I could be real
with the guy I was with, and that caused a lot of confusion for me. I liked
being taken care of but hated it at the same time. It reminded me of my
dad, who controlled everything in my life.

Both Amelia and Nick acknowledged that their unsatisfying relationships stemmed in part from familiar patterns they had learned in their narcissistic families. They each worked on their recovery and on changing the unhealthy dynamic they had grown up with. Eventually, they both found partners with whom they could be interdependent, respectful, and mutually loving.

Trust

As we've discussed in previous chapters, impaired trust is a consequence of growing up in a narcissistic family. It is important to share this information with your current partner or any potential new partner. There is no need to feel ashamed of this truth about yourself. If your partner or potential partner cares about you, they will be open to learning that your difficulty trusting someone is something you're aware of and are working to change. If your partner knows you are working on it, and are willing to address it, it will become less of a problem in the relationship.

If your lack of trust is causing problems in the relationship, it's a great time to do some couples counseling with a therapist skilled in understanding narcissistic family dynamics. It's far more workable and treatable than it may seem, when everyone understands what is going on.

Emotional Intimacy

Another aspect of a healthy love relationship that was likely missing in our narcissistic families is emotional intimacy. Emotional intimacy in a love relationship requires vulnerability and empathy. This means sharing your authentic feelings and your partner doing the same. It also involves practicing the same empathic rules in your relationship that we discussed for empathic parenting:

+ Identifying each person's feelings
+ Checking back to make sure each of you understands the other's expressed feelings
+ Acknowledging and empathizing with each other's feelings
+ Working to solve the problem that elicited those feelings

Attraction to a Partner's Essential Qualities

What are the essential qualities in a healthy attraction to another individual? When we were teenagers, it seemed like physical chemistry was at the core of our attraction to someone, but as adults we know better. A strong and healthy attraction will likely be a combination of physical, intellectual, emotional, and spiritual qualities—as well as having similar interests (and maybe similar politics, these days) and a personality that we find compelling or interesting. Finally, what is most crucial is how our authentic character and values mesh with those of our partner or potential partner. Growing up in a narcissistic family, we were likely not taught to focus on a person's character and values. As adults, we can be mindful of the fact that although we may be physically and intellectually attracted to someone who also has a great personality, if their character and core values are at odds with ours, the relationship will not necessarily be strong or healthy.

Journal Topics and Questions on Love Relationships

+ Write about patterns in your love relationships. Do you tend to be dependent or codependent? Both or neither?
+ Do you have shame concerning your relationship patterns? Assess where you need to forgive yourself, and write about self-compassion.
+ Write about interdependence in your love relationships.
+ Write about how you feel when you're with your partner.
+ Does your partner bring out the best and most authentic you?
• Are there trust issues in your relationship? Write about your concerns.
+ Write about how you are practicing empathy in your relationship.
+ Write about the essentials of your attraction to your partner.

♦ Write about core values that you share with your partner.

♦ If you are not in a relationship, write about the ideal relationship for you.

Friendships

Often adult children from narcissistic families struggle with friendships in similar ways that they struggle with love relationships. If you grew up with a narcissistic parent, not only will you tend to attract and be attracted to a narcissistic partner, you may also find yourself with narcissists as friends. Again, this ongoing connection to narcissists can be attributed to our being unintentionally drawn to a familiar family dynamic. Acknowledging that our friendships may be similar to unhealthy relationships in our narcissistic families can be difficult, because often we must let go of those friendships in order to complete our recovery.

Let's look at some common themes in healthy and unhealthy friendships:

Setting Boundaries

If you have friends who have narcissistic traits, you may find yourself having to set new boundaries in order to protect yourself. For example, if your friend wants to talk for long hours on the phone when you are clearly busy, you will need to kindly say that you have to work and can only talk for a short period of time. Or perhaps your friend wants to go out to a movie and stay out late, and you are too tired to do that. You simply state that you are not available but can do it another time when you feel better.

Setting boundaries may cause you to fear that your friend will no longer understand or respect you, no longer like you, or possibly even abandon you. It's important, however, to commit to setting boundaries; otherwise, you'll find yourself in an unhealthy pattern not unlike that of the family dynamic you're recovering from. A good friend will respect and understand your need to set boundaries.

Reciprocity

If you grew up in a narcissistic family, you likely did not experience much reciprocity in your family relationships. It is now time to be ultra-aware of the importance of reciprocity in all your connections.

Do you find you are always the giver in your friendships? Are you always the one who makes the initial call to connect or get together? Are you the thoughtful one who always remembers to check on your friend when they're not feeling well or are going through something difficult, only to be hurt when such thoughtfulness is never reciprocated? Is your friend continually and overly bossy—not just suggesting what you *might* do, but telling you what you *should* do? Is there an equal balance of give and take in your friendship? Or do you feel uncomfortable with the lack of reciprocity in the relationship?

You may find that you have attracted a narcissist as a friend and are suddenly in a position of deciding if that person is someone with whom you want to continue a friendship.

Jealousy

Adult children of narcissists have usually dealt with jealousy in their family of origin. The narcissistic parent may have been jealous of your relationship with the enabling or other parent. Siblings who grew up in a narcissistic family still may be competitive with each other and unable to share in each other's successes or accomplishments.

Is the theme of jealousy popping up in your friendships? For a friendship to be authentic and healthy, it's important to be able to share your struggles and successes without fearing that your friend will be jealous. A good friend will be empathetic with your struggles but also be there to celebrate your achievements.

Empathy

Empathy—the ability to tune in to another's feelings and validate and acknowledge those feelings—is essential in a strong, healthy friendship. But adult children from narcissistic families may be so used to not receiving empathic treatment from their parents and/or siblings that they may accept friendships in which this important quality is lacking. Are you finding that the people you hang out with are unable to empathize with you? When you choose to become friends with someone, do you consider that person's ability to be empathetic? Those who have this ability are priceless—and keepers!

Journal Topics and Questions on Friendships

♦ Write about any concerns you have about your friendships.
♦ Write about the friends with whom you can be your authentic self.
♦ Write about whether or not your friends give you empathy when you feel the need for it.
♦ Write about whether or not your friends celebrate your successes.
♦ Write about whether or not your friends appreciate the real you.
♦ Write about whether or not your friends bring out the best in you.
♦ Write about how you feel when you're with particular friends.
♦ Write about whether or not the give-and-take between you and your friends is essentially equal.
♦ Write about attempts to set boundaries with your friends.
♦ Write about unhealthy friendships that you may have to decide to part with.
♦ Write about your own ability to be a good friend.

Unlearning Narcissistic Traits

If you grew up in a narcissistic family, you could have learned some narcissistic traits. This does not mean that you are a narcissist. If there are some narcissistic traits you think you have learned from your family, you can decide to work on those traits in your recovery.

The following is a version of the nine narcissistic traits listed in the *DSM* (*Diagnostic and Statistical Manual of Mental Disorders*). Ask yourself these questions in order to assess whether or not you may be struggling with certain narcissistic traits. You might see some areas of growth you'll want to work on, and that's okay.

♦ Do I exaggerate my accomplishments and say I have done things I have not done? Do I act as if I am more important than others?

♦ Am I unrealistic about my thoughts and desires regarding love, beauty, success, intelligence? Do I seek power in these things?

♦ Do I believe that I am so special and unique that only the best institutions and the highest academic professionals could possibly understand me?

♦ Do I need to be admired all the time to the point of excess?

♦ Do I have a sense of entitlement and expect to be treated differently and with more status than others?

♦ Do I exploit others to get what I want or need?

♦ Do I lack empathy and therefore never see what others are feeling or needing? Or can I put myself in other people's shoes? Can I show empathy?

♦ Am I jealous and competitive with others, or do I unreasonably, without logic, think that others are jealous of me?

♦ Am I a haughty person who acts arrogant and "better than" with my friends, colleagues, and family?

You might also want to refer to the original list of narcissistic traits from the *DSM*, which are found in the appendix of this book.

As we have discussed throughout this book, if you are able to empathize and emotionally tune in to others, rest assured that you are not a narcissist.

Journal Topics and Questions on Self-Assessment of Narcissistic Traits

♦ Look at the *DSM* traits in the appendix, and journal about any of them you think you may be struggling with or want to work on.

♦ Write about your ability to provide empathy and emotionally tune in to other people's feelings.

♦ Write about your own self-acceptance and what that looks like for you.

♦ Write about your own accountability.

Completing the Recovery Work

You have now either read through the recovery work section of this book in order to get the big picture and are ready to go back and work the steps, or you have already begun to work the steps and are on your own recovery journey. It is important to give yourself credit for the hard work you have accomplished. Save your journal so that you can go back and assess how far you have come.

This recovery work is a lifelong journey; there may be times you will fall back and have to repeat a step, and that's perfectly normal and okay. You have opened yourself up to a new and fearless way of thinking about and understanding your family history, and to living a new life of freedom from your past.

It is my hope that you now comprehend the dynamic of the narcissistic family system and recognize the ways in which it affected you. You have the tools for recovery. I encourage you to be faithful to your own values and to maintain the courage to stand in your own truth and be your authentic self.

My heart will always be with you.

Notes

1. https://www.britannica.com/topic/Gaslight-film-by-Cukor.
2. https://www.thesun.co.uk/news/6006140/internet-child-shaming-parents/.
3. Karyl McBride, Ph.D., *Will I Ever Be Good Enough?* (New York: Free Press, 2008), back cover quote from Nanette Gartrell, M.D.
4. Stephanie Donaldson-Pressman and Robert Pressman, *The Narcissistic Family* (New York: Lexington Books, 1994), 18.
5. Elan Golomb, Ph.D., *Trapped in the Mirror: Adult Children of Narcissists in Their Struggle for Self* (New York: William Morrow, 1992), 180.
6. https://www.verywellmind.com/erik-eriksons-stages-of-psychosocial-development-2795740.
7. Stephanie Donaldson-Pressman and Robert Pressman, *The Narcissistic Family* (New York: Lexington Books, 1994), 14.
8. Amir Levine and Rachel Heller, *Attached: The New Science of Adult Attachment and How It Can Help You Find—and Keep—Love* (New York: Tarcher-Perigee, 2012).
9. Murray Bowen, *Family Therapy in Clinical Practice* (New York: Jason Aronson, 1978), 539.
10. Ibid., 53–42.
11. Julie L. Hall, *The Narcissist in Your Life* (New York: Lifelong Books, 2019), 173.
12. https://www.goodreads.com/author/quotes/269803.Ethel_Waters.
13. http://www.twainquotes.com/Self_approval.html.
14. American Psychiatric Association, *Diagnostic and Statistical Manual of Mental Disorders*, 5th Edition: *DSM-5*.

15. www.webmd.com/mental-health/what-to-know-complex-ptsd-symptoms.

16. Ibid.

17. Ibid.

18. Van der Kolk, Bessel. *The Body Keeps the Score: Brain, Mind, and Body in the Healing of Trauma.* New York: Penguin Books, 2015, p. 30.

19. https://drarielleschwartz.com/the-neurobiology-of-trauma-dr-arielle-schwartz/#.YTS_EI5KiM8.

20. Bruce D. Perry and John Marcellus, "The Impact of Abuse and Neglect on the Developing Brain," Scholastic.com, http://teacher.scholastic.com/professional/bruceperry/abuse_neglect.htm.

21. https://practicenotes.org/v17n2/brain.htm, referencing B. Perry, R. Pollard, T. Blakley, W. Baker, and D. Vigilante, "Childhood Trauma, the Neurobiology of Adaptation, and 'Use-Dependent' Development of the Brain: How 'States' Become 'Traits,'" *Infant Mental Health Journal* 16, no. 4 (1995): 271–91.

22. Elisabeth Kübler-Ross, M.D., *On Death and Dying* (New York: Macmillan, 1969).

23. The picture frame and gift box were helpful ideas from Stephanie Donaldson-Pressman and Robert M. Pressman, *The Narcissistic Family: Diagnosis and Treatment* (San Francisco, CA: Jossey-Bass, 1994), which I have adapted to our recovery model.

24. You can watch my YouTube video of the Giraffe Club at this link: https://www.youtube.com/watch?v=TplqWrya_Kg (Giraffe Story by Dr. Karyl McBride).

25. Lewis Smedes, *Shame and Grace: Healing the Shame We Don't Deserve* (San Francisco: HarperCollins, 1993).

Narcissistic Personality Disorder Diagnostic Criteria

Source: American Psychiatric Association: *Diagnostic and Statistical Manual of Mental Disorders*, Fifth Edition (Arlington, VA: American Psychiatric Association, 2013), 66–70.

A pervasive pattern of grandiosity (in fantasy or behavior), need for admiration, and lack of empathy, beginning by early adulthood and present in a variety of contexts, as indicated by five (or more) of the following:

1. Has a grandiose sense of self-importance (e.g., exaggerates achievements and talents, expects to be recognized as superior without commensurate achievements).
2. Is preoccupied with fantasies of unlimited success, power, brilliance, beauty, or ideal love.
3. Believes that he or she is "special" and unique and can only be understood by, or should associate with, other special or high-status people (or institutions).
4. Requires excessive admiration.
5. Has a sense of entitlement (i.e., unreasonable expectations of especially favorable treatment or automatic compliance with his or her expectations).
6. Is interpersonally exploitative (i.e., takes advantage of others to achieve his or her own ends).
7. Lacks empathy: is unwilling to recognize or identify with the feelings and needs of others.
8. Is often envious of others or believes that others are envious of him or her.
9. Shows arrogant, haughty behaviors or attitudes.

Recommended Reading

Beattie, Melody. *Beyond Codependency: And Getting Better All the Time*. Center City, MN: Hazelden Foundation, 1989.

Behary, Wendy T. *Disarming the Narcissist*. Oakland, CA: New Harbinger Publications, 2021.

Bowlby, John. *A Secure Base: Parent-Child Attachment and Healthy Human Development*. Philadelphia, PA: Basic Books, 1988.

Brown, Nina W. *Children of the Self-Absorbed: A Grown-Up's Guide to Getting Over Narcissistic Parents*. Oakland, CA: New Harbinger, 2001.

Burgo, Joseph. *The Narcissist You Know: Defending Yourself Against Extreme Narcissists in an All-About-Me Age*. New York: Simon & Schuster, 2015.

Campbell, Keith. *The New Science of Narcissism: Understanding One of the Greatest Psychological Challenges of Our Time—and What You Can Do About It*. Sounds True, 2020.

Donaldson-Pressman, Stephanie, and Robert M. Pressman. *The Narcissistic Family: Diagnosis and Treatment*. San Francisco, CA: Jossey-Bass, 1997.

Forward, Susan. *Toxic Parents: Overcoming Their Hurtful Legacy and Reclaiming Your Life*. New York: Bantam, 1989.

Gibson, Lindsay C. *Adult Children of Emotionally Immature Parents*. Oakland, CA: New Harbinger Publications, 2015.

Golomb, Elan. *Trapped in the Mirror: Adult Children of Narcissists in Their Struggle for Self*. New York: William Morrow, 1992.

Gottman, John. *Raising an Emotionally Intelligent Child: The Heart of Parenting*. New York: Simon & Schuster, 1998.

Herman, Judith, *Trauma and Recovery: The Aftermath of Violence from Domestic Abuse to Political Terror*. New York: Basic Books, 1997.

Hotchkiss, Sandy. *Why Is It Always About You? Saving Yourself from the Narcissists in Your Life*. New York: Simon & Schuster, 2002.

Kreisman, Jerold and Hal Straus. *I Hate You—Don't Leave Me: Understanding the Borderline Personality*. New York: Penguin Random House, 2010.

Lerner, Rokelle. *The Object of My Affection Is in My Reflection: Coping with Narcissists*. Deerfield Beach, FL: HCI Books, 2008.

Levine, Amir and Rachel Heller, *Attached: The New Science of Adult Attachment and How It Can Help You Find—and Keep—Love*. New York: TarcherPerigee, 2012.

Lowen, Alexander. *Narcissism: Denial of the True Self*. New York: Touchstone, 1985.

Masterson, James F. *The Search for the Real Self: Unmasking the Personality Disorders of Our Age*. New York: Simon & Schuster, 1988.

McBride, Karyl. *Will I Ever Be Free of You?: How to Navigate a High-Conflict Divorce from a Narcissist and Heal Your Family*. New York: Simon & Schuster, 2014.

McBride, Karyl. *Will I Ever Be Good Enough?: Healing the Daughters of Narcissistic Mothers*. New York: Simon & Schuster, 2008.

Miller, Alice. *The Drama of the Gifted Child: The Search for the True Self*, 3rd edition. New York: HarperCollins, 1996.

Minuchin, Salvador. *Families and Family Therapy*. Cambridge, MA: Harvard University Press, 1974.

Neff, Kristin. *Self-Compassion*. New York: William Morrow, 2011.

Paul, Jordan, and Margaret Paul. *Do I Have to Give Up Me to Be Loved by You?*, 2nd edition. Center City, MN: Hazelden, 2002; Philadelphia: Westminster Press, 1983.

Perry, Bruce D., M.D., Ph.D., and Maia Szalavitz, *The Boy Who Was Raised as a Dog: And Other Stories from a Child Psychiatrist's Notebook—What Traumatized Children Can Teach Us About Loss, Love, and Healing*. New York: Basic Books, 2017.

Perry, Bruce D., M.D., Ph.D., and Oprah Winfrey. *What Happened to You?: Conversations on Trauma, Resilience, and Healing*. New York: Flatiron Books, 2021.

Secunda, Victoria. *When Madness Comes Home: Help and Hope for Families of the Mentally Ill*. New York: Hyperion Books, 1998.

Stern, Robin. *The Gaslight Effect: How to Spot and Survive the Hidden Manipulation Others Use to Control Your Life*. New York: Harmony Books, 2018.

Szalavitz, Maia, and Bruce D. Perry. *Born for Love: Why Empathy Is Essential— and Endangered*. New York: William Morrow, 2010.

Ulanov, Ann and Barry. *Cinderella and Her Sisters: The Envied and the Envying*.

Van Der Kolk, Bessel A. *The Body Keeps the Score*. New York: Penguin Random House, 2014.

Sexual Abuse Resources

Bass, Ellen, and Laura Davis. *The Courage to Heal: A Guide for Women Survivors of Child Sexual Abuse*. New York: Harper & Row Publishers, 1988.

Davis, Laura. *The Courage to Heal Workbook: For Women and Men Survivors of Child Sexual Abuse*. New York: Harper & Row Publishers, 1990.

Hindman, Jan. *Just Before Dawn: From the Shadows of Tradition to New Reflections in Trauma Assessment and Treatment of Sexual Victimization*. Ontario, Oregon: AlexAndria Associates, 1989.

Leberg, Eric. *Understanding Child Molesters: Taking Charge*. Thousand Oaks, CA: Sage Publications, 1997.

Terr, Lenore. *Too Scared to Cry: Psychic Trauma in Childhood*. New York: Harper & Row Publishers, 1990.

Wiehe, Vernon R. *Sibling Abuse: Hidden Physical, Emotional, and Sexual Trauma*. New York: Lexington Books, 1990.

Index

About the Author

Karyl McBride, Ph.D., is one of the leading authorities on the topic of narcissism and a licensed marriage and family therapist in Denver, Colorado, with forty-plus years of experience in public and private practice. She specializes in treating couples, families, children, and individuals with dysfunctional family issues, including trauma and divorce.

For over twenty years, Dr. McBride has been researching and treating narcissism in families and in intimate relationships. She is the author of *Will I Ever Be Good Enough?: Healing the Daughters of Narcissistic Mothers* and *Will I Ever Be Free of You?: How to Navigate a High-Conflict Divorce from a Narcissist and Heal Your Family*.

Dr. McBride's work has been featured in numerous magazines, newspapers, websites, and radio and television shows, including the *New York Times* Well Book Club, *Elle*, *Maclean's*, and *Dr. Phil*. She is a contributing expert blogger for PsychologyToday.com and has also written for the *Huffington Post*. She can be found online at willieverbegoodenough.com, KarylMcBridePhD.com, Facebook.com/DrKarylMcBride, as well as on LinkedIn and Twitter.

To contact Dr. McBride for speaking engagements, media, workshops, or further information, email her at karyl@drmcbride.com.